Louise Harrison McCran

Eph. 2:10

JAMES H. McCONKEY

JAMES H. McCONKEY

A MAN OF GOD

By
LOUISE HARRISON McCRAW
Author, "Glorious Triumph," "Blue Skies," etc.

SECOND EDITION

ZONDERVAN PUBLISHING HOUSE
GRAND RAPIDS   MICHIGAN

EIGHT-FIFTEEN FRANKLIN STREET
GRAND RAPIDS, MICHIGAN

PREFACE

AFTER the shock that accompanied the news of Mr. McConkey's Home-going (for it is always a shock, no matter how long the preparation may have been) my first reaction was that of gratitude to God for allowing me the privilege of setting down, in order, some of the events in his life, of attempting to explain the secret of power in that life. If our association had been stretched over a longer period, doubtless this would have been a larger book; there would have been more incidents recorded. However, I trust that the Lord has brought to my remembrance sufficient to prove to all who read this, one thing: in James McConkey, that is, in his flesh, dwelt no good thing, but Christ lived in him—and this is quite enough! Left to himself, he would have been, doubtless, a gentleman distinguished for intelligence, kindness, and culture, and perhaps for success in some chosen career, but spiritually, he would have been as sounding brass and a tinkling cymbal. If at any point, the author seems to have fallen short in drawing clearly the line between human and Divine, natural and spiritual, let it be recognized as an unwitting error of the head and not of the heart—that through it all the man may be recognized only as an instrument, but that instrument which the Lord Jesus Christ used to bring the writer into His very presence!

It will be apparent to all who read, no doubt, that the making of this biography would have been humanly impossible but for the coöperation of Mr. McConkey's relatives and many of his close friends, who have been most kind in furnishing incidents and suggestions. Their names appear on various pages of the book, and to each, the author is profoundly grateful.

In view of the fact that Mr. McConkey left no immediate family, one of his nephews, Mr. W. McConkey Kerr, kindly consented to represent the McConkey family in the matter of editing the manuscript. With painstaking care, Mr. Kerr went over each page, each word, making changes, eliminations and additions. Many of the sentences are his expressions and several entire paragraphs were written by him. It was at his suggestion that many of the quotations from Mr. McConkey's books and tracts were included as he felt that some who might read these pages would be constrained thereby to go further into such reading. It was his privilege to know his uncle very intimately. This close, personal relationship combined with his training and experience has peculiarly fitted Mr. Kerr for the task of editing Mr. McConkey's life story.

Before the manuscript was sent to the publishers, it was read carefully by Dr. Henry W. Frost, whose own literary skill and spiritual insight have made his suggestions of inestimable worth. Because of the value of their services, I wish to express publicly to both Dr. Frost and Mr. Kerr my sincere appreciation of their help.

L. H. M.

INTRODUCTION

THOSE of us who are familiar with the writings of James McConkey will have noted the fact that they have a vigorous quality about them not usually characterizing the literary productions of highly spiritual men. They are declarative without being argumentative, and strong without being dogmatic; for James, like his predecessor, James the Just, was no weakling. On the contrary, he was strongly convinced as to God's truth and fearless in his expressions concerning it. One, therefore, cannot read his pamphlets and books without feeling that here is a man of faith whose beliefs are well worth sharing, and a man of courage whose bold and steadfast way is well worth following. There are men who impart newness of life to those who are weary and out of the way: James McConkey was one of them.

And yet there was an anomaly of life in our brother and friend the like of which is not often seen among men. This strong man was as lowly-minded as a child and as tender-hearted as a woman. There are some of us who have felt his arms encircle our neck, and his cheek laid against our cheek and have heard his vibrant greeting, "My beloved!", and this without the least suggestion of effeminacy, but conveying the impression that here was a Mr. Greatheart whose love could not be restrained. This tenderness was in all he said and did. It was in his face, in the tone of his voice, in the touch of his hand, in the actions of his life. 'Way back in college days this was true, and in later life it was conspicuously true. It was his nature from the first, but it became his new nature as he learned to practice companionship with the gentle Christ and became more and more like Him. James

Introduction

McConkey loved everyone, particularly those who were of the household of faith; and conversely, everyone loved him. It is strange that he never married for he needed the strengthening and comforting of a woman companion, and he had the heart to make such an one supremely happy. He told me, once, that he did not know why he had not married. I judge that he was not set against marriage but was preoccupied with his work and especially with his Lord. Perhaps we gained as a result of this. At any rate, he gave all the love he had, which was infinitely great, to his friends and the world at large.

The hour came when his earthly work was done. For seven long and weary years, as a result of a broken hip, he had lain in his bed or in an invalid's chair and this without complaining. And at last came the heavenly call, the closing of the eyes in sleep, and the passing into those eternal habitations of which he had thought, written, and spoken so much. How the trumpets must have sounded as he arrived triumphantly home! And how his heart must have thrilled as he looked upon the face of Him who had been his all in all and in Whose Name he had valiantly conquered! Who then could wish him back to that bed of pain and away from those infinite and eternal joys! Yea, we who loved him well and long to see him again are willingly separated from him until the shadows pass from our lives as they have passed from his.

HENRY W. FROST
Director Emeritus of the China Inland Mission
(Mr. McConkey's classmate at Princeton University, and his abiding friend)

CONTENTS

"There was a man sent from God . . ."
　　　　　　　　　　—St. John 1: 6

I

AS THE TWIG IS BENT

THERE are hero-worshipers who deplore the debunking tendency of this age, but sane realists recognize the fact that, if the world is to get at the truth about personalities, a certain amount of debunking must be done. The question is, Who is to do it? Nearly nineteen centuries ago a saint of God wrote under inspiration, "If we judged ourselves, we should not be judged," and occasionally a man is found who applies this truth to himself.

One winter, when James H. McConkey was on his annual visit to Richmond, Virginia, a young lady, who was very devoted to him and followed all his speaking engagements, became irritated because of an introduction given him by the acting assistant pastor of the old Trinity Methodist Church. There was an unusually large congregation that Sunday morning, due partly to the fact that Glenna James, a senior from Westhampton College, had made it her business to bring a large delegation of college girls across the city to hear a man whose books had meant something vital in her life. A thrill of expectancy passed over the congregation, but when the assistant pastor rose to introduce the visitor, he seemed to find nothing to say

11

except, "Our speaker for this morning is Mr. James H. McConkey, of Pittsburgh."

Afterwards the loyal friend, who always listened jealously to every word of the introductions, said to Mr. McConkey, "Mr. —————— made me tired this morning. These ministers never do say enough about you."

His reply was: "Oh yes, my minister friends are very kind. They always say enough—too much usually. But you know, I had a dentist friend to present me once, and his introduction suited me better than any of the rest. All he said was, "This is an old piece of clay that the Lord works through!"

There it is! All claims denied except to clay! There is no need for us to go further into unearthing his weaknesses. Everyone realizes the worthlessness of clay in itself. It is only the potter who deserves credit. Often when he quoted with half-closed eyes, "I know that in me, that is, in my flesh, dwelleth no good thing," we wondered if Paul himself could have said it with more intensity of realization. And since he was only clay, and since no good thing dwelt in his flesh, it would be entirely illogical to sound one note of praise of James McConkey. However, as we cast our eyes back upon his life, doubtless, we shall be praising God continually for His gifts to this man and for his use of those gifts after they had been yielded to Him.

There was, however, in his early life, no special yielding and no special consciousness of heaven's favor. Like the average boy, he accepted his heritage as a matter of course. Later he must have thanked his God upon every remembrance of his honorable ancestry and the luxurious surroundings in which his boyhood was spent. Perhaps in after years the Lord used this easy assurance of social position to give *entree* into otherwise difficult circles, and most probably it was an influential factor in preventing any trace of snobbery to develop in his nature. Like the typical gentleman, he acted on the assumption that there were none above him and none below! This was a natural gift but none the less a gift of God.

The McConkeys were one of the first families of the section of Pennsylvania contiguous to Lancaster and York, their Scotch-Irish ancestors having settled in Lancaster County in 1756. The first William McConkey, who was a great-grand uncle of James, was an intimate friend of Washington, and it was his home at Washington Crossing, above Trenton, in which the General spent the night before crossing the Delaware on December 25, 1776. All down the line the heads of the families were prominent in business, state and church affairs. William McConkey, the father of James, left Peach Bottom, where he had been brought up, and settled in Wrightsville, which town, by the way, missed being chosen as the Capital of the United States by just one vote. Here he was engaged in a large mercantile business, became one of the owners of the Aurora Furnace, president of the First National Bank, and represented York County in the legislature in 1855.

At 200 Front Street in a big, plain, brick house with a queer little porch at one end facing the Susquehanna River, thirteen children were born to William and his wife, Susan Ruth Silver. The seventh of these was James Henry, named for his grandfather, born February 15, 1858. Four died in infancy, leaving

Caroline, Elizabeth, Martha, Julia, Susan, James, Margaret, Edwin, and Blanche.

It was while the family lived in this house that General John B. Gordon with his twenty-eight hundred Confederate troops invaded the town, three days before the battle of Gettysburg. Several hours previous to this, the Union troops had burned the bridge, the bridge fired the lumber yards, the burning lumber fired the town, and General Gordon, with his characteristic chivalry, helped to save private property. James McConkey, then a boy of six, little knew that the Reverend John B. Gordon, of Richmond, a relative and namesake of this same General Gordon, would later become one of his dearly beloved friends, when war-time prejudices were wiped out and both were one in Christ.

In 1875 the family residence was transferred to a very imposing red brick mansion of fifteen rooms built by the father nearer the center of town. This house, set back a short distance from the street with its full-length porch, its white pillars, its three stories—all with high ceilings and inside blinds—is still one of the most handsome in Wrightsville. It was in the spacious, oblong parlor, with the tapestried library at the back, that the family orchestra played, James leading with the violin. Just across the wide hall was the living-room with the dining-room back of it, and joining that the kitchen where, occasionally, the children with a few of their intimate friends were allowed to take part in a square dance while the father played the violin. But James did not indulge, not because of scruples, but somehow even a square dance was not in keeping with his quiet, studious nature; and from his youth up, he unconsciously avoided discords.

His outstanding characteristics were inherited from the gentle, retiring mother rather than from the aggressive, public-spirited father. He adored her and never grew weary of extolling Christian motherhood, for he recognized her as the finest embodiment of this ideal. Susan Silver had left her old home, Silver Mount, in Harford County, Maryland, at the age of nineteen to enter seriously the career of home-making, and indeed the task of bringing up nine children in the nurture and admonition of the Lord was a life work not to be despised.

As a boy, James was just like any other boy, only more quiet and reserved, not given to pranks. He was very fond of baseball and fishing, and many a time his tall, slender form would be seen creeping stealthily along the top of the dam of the Susquehanna in search of rockfish. The fish would come near the dam and if the fisher wore rubber boots he might go near enough to cast the fly and bring in a good catch. But this was before he heard the call to become a fisher of men!

During his boyhood he showed no special promise of becoming a spiritual leader, and it was not until he reached young manhood that any profession of faith in Christ was made. He went to Sunday school (Miss Ella Lloyd from Albany, New York, was his teacher) and church as a matter of course, but his boyish heart was set, not toward things eternal, but things temporal.

At the age of eighteen he entered LaFayette College, matriculating August 31, 1876. He roomed in Number 4, McKeen Hall; but for some reason he changed to

Princeton College the following year and was gradu-
ated from that institution in the class of 1880. The
fact that he entered as a sophomore might have impaired his popularity, but evidently not, for he was
elected president of the class, which position he held
throughout his course and for seventeen years afterwards. In regard to this, Dr. Henry W. Frost says:

"All of this was the more remarkable as there was
nothing in McConkey to appeal to the usual sentiment
of college men. He was not an athlete; he was not
even a good mixer. He moved to and fro quietly,
almost sedately, though the smile upon his face and
the kindliness in his tone of voice indicated that he
was no separatist. In ways almost unknown to us and
altogether unknown to himself, he became a leader
among us, and when we wanted good, sane advice about
class and college affairs, we turned instinctively to
him. There was, even in those early days, a good deal
of the rock about him. He was solid, unshakable,
dependable.

"But it is not to be understood that James, in his
college days, was preëminent as a Christian. He was
a member of the Philadelphian Society and, along with
Jackson and Janvier, was a clear voice in the college
wilderness which called to manly and decent living.
Everyone knew that he was a Christian but few thought
of him as headed for a ministerial or missionary career.
A curious episode which happened later in his and
my life illustrates this:

"In the year 1895, I was visiting China and was
resident in our mission home in Shanghai. At the particular time in mind, I was sitting in my bedroom and
talking with a Mr. Lewis, who was one of our North

American missionaries from Philadelphia. Suddenly he said, 'Mr. Frost, is your name Jack?'

" 'Well,' I replied, 'it depends upon the men you may be talking with. If you would meet any of my college classmates, you would not hear me spoken of by any other name than Jack.'

"Then Mr. Lewis asked, 'Did you go to Princeton College?'

" 'Yes, I did!'

" 'Did you know James McConkey?'

" 'If you mean our classmate, Jim, I certainly did.'

"Then it was my turn to ask questions. I said, 'Where is James? And what is he doing?'

"My companion replied, 'He is giving Bible readings.'

" 'Giving Bible readings!' I exclaimed. 'I am astonished beyond measure.'

" 'That's curious,' said Lewis, 'that's what he said when I told him that you were a Bible teacher.'

"This meant that neither of us at Princeton had been pronounced in our Christian testimony."

The three years spent at Princeton were very happy ones for Jim McConkey. He loved the scholastic atmosphere of the place with all its rich associations. He enjoyed his intimate friends, but books were his first love; study, his first consideration. He was known primarily as a student. In the class just ahead of him—the famous class of 1879—he had a friend whom the boys called Tom, but whom the world came to know as T. Woodrow Wilson. (Mr. Wilson dropped his first name, Thomas, as soon as he became a writer.) Those who have read the booklet, *Holy Ground*, will remember Mr. McConkey's mention of their meeting in Pittsburgh, years afterward, during Mr. Wilson's second term as Chief Executive; of Mr. McConkey's contentment in "the little two-room office" God had given him for the carrying on of his God-given work; of his inability to envy President Wilson; his profound thankfulness to God for leading him into the work that had been foreordained for him.

As he walked alone under the Princeton elms and considered the legal career ahead, his heart leaped high at the thought of possible honors to be his in the future. He possessed a lawyer's brain and the lawyer's passion for logic, which, coupled with a lawyer's training and indomitable energy, might accomplish almost anything. Yes, he would go back to the city of York, just twelve miles from Wrightsville, and make the name of McConkey more illustrious in that community than ever before. This was his dream.

He was a member of Whig Hall at Princeton, and was successor to Woodrow Wilson as president of this society. There he debated with many men who were later to become famous in their profession. He had the honor of winning a debate over Robert McCarter, who subsequently became one of the greatest corporation lawyers in the country. In those days, Whig and Clio Halls were debating societies between which the keenest rivalry prevailed, the only secret organizations at Princeton. The Halls still exist in the beautiful and stately simplicity of their architecture, but they are no longer secret societies.

In December of his senior year, a blow came that shattered all his plans—the first tragic break in the family circle. William McConkey, devoted, indulgent husband and father, was stricken with a fatal illness.

His death left James, the eldest son, as the logical head of the house. There seemed nothing for him to do but go home and take up the burden of responsibility that was now his plain duty. He continued his studies at home, however, and returned to Princeton for his final examinations, which he passed most creditably, graduating fourth or fifth in his class.

As the narrative of his life unfolds, we shall see how James McConkey became a great overcomer through prayer and the power of the Holy Spirit, Who was his constant and unfailing companion through the years. In the tract, *Beauty for Ashes,* he relates how the Lord helped him to overcome the demon that is so prevalent in our high-pressure business world. Worry threatened to shorten his life as it did his father's.

"I recall an experience in my own Christian life. My father was dying of a disease brought on by worriment. A great physician had been summoned from the city. He was closeted with my father for a long time. Then he came out of the sick chamber soberly shaking his head. There was no hope. My father's race was run. Then my dear mother asked the great doctor to take me aside for a conference. For I myself was breaking in body, and from the same dread enemy which overthrows so many Christians—anxious care. So the kind-hearted physician took me into the parlor, and we sat down for a heart-to-heart chat. Very searchingly and with all the skill of an expert did he draw forth from me the humiliating fact that I was a prey of worriment and suffering from its dread results. Then he turned to me and in a few, keen, incisive sentences with no attempt at concealment, told me that I had fallen a victim to the same habit which had been my father's undoing, and that unless I overcame it, there was no hope for me even as there was none for him.

"I went upstairs. I threw myself upon my knees in my bedchamber. I cried out in my agony of soul— 'Oh, Christ! He says I must overcome worriment. And Thou alone knowest how I have tried to do so. I have fought. I have struggled. I have wept bitter tears. And I have failed. O Lord Jesus, unless Thou dost undertake for me now it is all over with me!' Then and there I threw myself in utter self-helplessness upon Christ. Somehow, where before I had been struggling I now found myself trusting as I had never quite done before. From that time onward Jesus Christ began to give me the beauty of victory for the sombre ashes of defeat!"

As best he could, he assumed his father's responsibility for an invalid mother, seven sisters and a brother of sixteen. If the old adage that a lawyer must starve two years before he can make a living were true, then law, for the present, was out of the question, although he took the State Bar examinations and was admitted to the bar in York. But the roseate dreams of practicing law must be put aside while the matter of an immediately profitable business was faced. Those familiar with *The Dedicated Life* know that a wholesale ice business was the result, that he and "another young man" (I. W. Miller), embarked all they had and considerably more in this venture. This partnership of McConkey and Miller continued for fifteen years.

Meantime things went on in the home as well as could be expected without the husband and father.

Mrs. McConkey considered James as head of the house, and he looked after her with as much tender solicitude as his father could have done, until her death in 1884. His room was next to hers, that she might call him at any time during the night if she needed him. Susan McConkey, large in body and spirit, had been faithful to her trust in rearing her family, and now laid aside by paralysis, she was patient in suffering. Through the long summer days she would sit in her invalid's chair in the shady yard, while neighboring children played around her; and Frances, the Irish cook who had been with the family for many years, went in and out attending to her duties.

This difficult period was the Lord's training-time; this situation, the crucible in which James's life was molded. In the beginning of it he knew very little of the meaning of "yielding" and "surrender"—terms which he used with so much harnessed force in later years; but he recognized plain duty and accepted it, and it was in this prosaic path of duty that the Lord spoke to him, as He did to Moses, while tending the sheep. But for the shattering of a cherished dream, and imposition of heavy and burdensome responsibilities which literally threw him on his God, he might have lived his life with no more impress of Christ upon his fellow-man than had been made at Princeton; but an infinitely wise Father looked down and saw that strong forces must be used to break the strong will of this man; that the man himself must be bruised, yea, broken, before he could be made a vessel fit for such holy and acceptable use as He had in mind. Very early in the bruising process came a failing in health— the wolf that came to destroy, mentioned in *The Sure*

Shepherd. He had made a public profession of faith in Christ at the age of twenty, and four years later he was made an elder in the church, which office he held as long as he lived. For years he was superintendent of the Sunday School, and it was during this period that he went abroad for his health. The following letter addressed to the teachers and pupils of his Sunday School, in care of Mr. Matthew Kerr, has been preserved:

"Nice, France
"Wednesday, December 10, 1884
"Dear Scholars and Teachers:

"I had hoped to be able to write you a letter from Germany, describing to you the Christmas customs of that country, for there, as with us at home, Christmas is the great day of the year. The climate, however, was so cold and raw that I was obliged to leave and come to Italy, and am thus unable to write you a description of a German Christmas. Nevertheless, I would be greatly disappointed if I could not hail you across the great ocean with a 'Merry Christmas to all!' so I am going to do so by letter.

"And first, let me thank you all for the many kind inquiries which I receive concerning my health. We had rather a rough passage across the Atlantic and I must frankly state that I missed a great many of my meals, and felt a good part of the time as though I were riding on that elegant 'Flying Horse' which our popular librarian sometimes puts up for us at our celebrations. Still, this feeling left me before the voyage ended, and I am now enjoying good health and have good reason to hope that I shall return entirely restored.

"I am among the Alps of southern France and quite close to the frontier of Italy. The country is very beautiful, indeed, far more so than you could imagine, or than I could picture to you. The railroad winds among the mountains and valleys and is lined with vineyards and olive, lemon, orange, and palm trees. The mountains are very grand and lofty, and the valleys, sunny and fertile. There are many interesting sights and many funny ones, too. You meet a big, two-story cart with a large load of hay hauled by a little donkey about the size of the ordinary American hobby-horse. Indeed, if the roads were not so smooth and hard as they are, it would be impossible for a donkey so laughingly small to haul such loads as they do.

"The people have the usual Italian dark complexion and black hair, are lively and excitable and chatter away like a lot of bluejays. Among the mountains, the peasants dress in bright, gay colors and seem to be equally gay and happy in disposition. The manners and customs of all these nations, are, of course, strange and unlike our own. Children are children the world over, however, and it is very pleasing to find the children so much like our own. For the little ones are merry, happy, and natural and always make one feel at home. In Germany the small schoolboys wear high-top boots, also little knapsacks in which they carry their books. Of course you can imagine how proud they feel when rigged out in this style, and they look like little soldiers as you meet them in the streets trooping home from school. This little story will show you that they, like all children, are very quick and bright in some of their sayings and doings:

"A party of four American boys, in tramping through

the mountains, met a little peasant lad who wanted to
go with them to the top of a certain mountain which
they were going to climb. In order to turn him back,
they began, as we say in America, to 'chaff' the little
fellow. They told him their company was very valuable, and that if he wanted to go with them, he would
have to pay them for the privilege. At this, young
Fritz took off his little cap, made a very polite bow,
pulled out his tiny purse and offered them a piece
of silver. Of course they refused—as he knew they
would—and he continued to follow them, being bound
to go to the summit. By and by, they thought they
would frighten him back so one of the four said: 'Fritz,
we eat all the small boys we meet. Would you like
to be eaten?' Again Fritz took off his cap, made his
bow, and replied very seriously, 'If you please, sir,
I would prefer being eaten *on top of the mountain!!!*'
I think he was as smart as a certain boy in Hellam
township, York County, who thought everybody ought
to know that blackberries were 'all aready' in October.

"They do not celebrate Christmas in Italy and France
as we do at home, and it makes one feel as though
such countries cannot be as happy as our own. I fear
I shall be somewhat homesick for my Sunday School
at Christmas-time, and will miss the sweet songs which
we have always sung together then. I will certainly
appreciate them to the full when I hear them again.

"A Merry Christmas then to you all! dear scholars
and teachers. May this day of holy memories be free
from all sickness and sorrow, and bring to each member of our beloved little school a wealth of joy and
happiness and purest pleasure. That the memory of
the sweet Christ-child, whose glorious birth we com-

memorate, may fill our hearts with tenderness and peace and good will, and that His everlasting and richest blessings may abide with you, is the earnest wish of "Your affectionate Superintendent,

"James H. McConkey"

His stay in Europe, where he traveled by bicycle through Germany, southern France, Italy, and Switzerland, was an experience he never forgot and one that colored his writings in after years. The matchless splendor of the Alps, the quiet beauty of southern France, and the historic grandeur of Italy, were meat and drink for his beauty-loving soul. But it had not been necessary to go so far away to find beautiful scenery, for it was all around in York and Lancaster Counties. He told an old friend at home that in all his travels he had seen nothing more beautiful than "Round Top," the little mountain two miles north of Wrightsville on the same side of the Susquehanna as the town.

One day on a railroad train in Switzerland, Mr. McConkey and a Scotch minister, with whom he had formed a friendship, noticed a beautiful young woman just across the aisle from them. Feeling sure she would not understand English, they began to tease each other about her—about trying to get an introduction to one so charming, while she was apparently unconscious of it all. This went on until her station was called, and then, just as she passed out to the platform, she waved a hand good-naturedly and said, "Good-by, Americans!"

This incident was unusual, not characteristic!

It is hard to record spiritual facts in chronological

order but during these fifteen years (from 1880 to 1895), James McConkey began to study his Bible under the instruction of the Holy Spirit. The responsibility of witnessing was laid upon him and, most of all, the duty and privilege of surrendering all he had, in fee simple, to the Lord Jesus Christ. To use his own phraseology, he had got all of Christ when he accepted and confessed Him, but Christ had not got all of him. Now he saw that nothing else would do. The exact date of his definite surrender of himself to the Lord has not been kept, but he says in *The Surrendered Life* that he had been a Christian, an officer in the church and a Sunday school superintendent for years, so it is natural to suppose that it came sometime after his trip abroad. He also says that as a result of the prayer that followed a consecration message he heard in a near-by city, he was strongly moved. The one sentence, "Lord, thou knowest we can trust the Man who died for us," stayed with him all the way home, and that night in the quiet of his room he definitely yielded every purpose and plan of his life, himself, to the Man who had died for him. The name of the speaker who was thus used of God to follow his message with this Spirit-breathed prayer, we do not know. He may have died in obscurity, but doubtless he will share in the reward given James McConkey for trophies won by him. And who would be more delighted than this Apostle of the Surrendered Life to share anything good?

The following Sunday, the transaction he had made in his prayer closet, was made public is the Presbyterian Church of Wrightsville—the same church he had attended since childhood.   Perhaps the church people wondered, that Sunday morning, why such an exemplary character as James McConkey should take a step like that. Little did the average church member know what it cost to yield that strong will. *Things* were not so hard to give up, but the *will* was different! And he knew in his heart of hearts that the will was what God had His eye upon. He understood what Tennyson meant by those familiar lines:

> *"Our wills are ours, we know not how,*
> *Our wills are ours to make them Thine."*

Perhaps that was why he made his consecration public, to seal the decision for himself, to enforce it, to make him remember that the neighbors were watching to see if he kept his agreement with God.

The word "surrender" has been used in certain religious groups to connote the giving up of pet sins by people, not necessarily saved, who thereby curry favor with God by such action. Some Christians dislike the word because it has been defined thus. But those who knew Mr. McConkey, even those who knew him merely through his books, realized that the word applied only to Christians; that it meant simply handing over the life to the One who had already bought it with His blood—the natural act of "delivering the goods" already paid for. It was not a second blessing, but only the fullness of the first; the one thing required of God before the life could be used by Him. During later years he often spoke of "eating" the Word, and once remarked that it took him fifteen years to eat Romans 12:1.* I do not remember hearing him say that this

---

* I beseech you therefore, brethren, by the mercies of God, that ye present your bodies a living sacrifice, holy, acceptable unto God, which is your reasonable service.

was his life-verse, but I can think of no other that fitted him quite so well.

There was no conspicuous Christian service immediately following this act of consecration. He went quietly on with the usual activities in Sunday school and church, using whatever opportunities came his way for witnessing to those in his own providentially-prescribed circles, among them, his brother Edwin, and his hired man, William. Yet there was a constantly deepening work of the Holy Spirit in his life, an ever-increasing illumination of the Scriptures and a growing testimony, for these follow complete surrender as the day the night.

II

WIDENING CIRCLES

FORTUNATELY the McConkey mansion did not go out of the family until after the death of his sister, Margaret, who had married Mr. D. S. Cook, of Wrightsville in 1898. Mr. Cook bought the old home shortly after their marriage, and they made it truly a home for "Brother Jim" as long as they lived. During the period from 1880 to 1897, three of the sisters—Elizabeth, Julia and Blanche, were married, but Elizabeth remained in the home for some years afterwards. She, James and the other three stayed on there until his sisters were all happily married and his brother established in business. It was fortunate for him that at least one of the sisters was in charge of the house until about the time he went to live in Pittsburgh.

The place was noted for its hospitality. One of its frequent guests was Miss Mattie Bell, a Southerner whom the McConkeys had come to know through her brother, their former pastor. In those days even young people in the South did not call each other by first names unless they were very intimate, and when Miss Bell first came to Wrightsville to visit, she thought it strange that James McConkey, along with his sisters,

called her "Mattie." She was several years older than
he, so she felt somewhat pleased by what appeared to
be an inference that she was younger. She had not
been used to calling young men whom she had just
met by their first names, so instead of addressing him
as "James" or "Jim," she said, "Mr. McConkey." He,
swift to defer to others in all matters non-essential, then
addressed her as "Miss Bell."

After fifteen or more years of apprenticeship in
business, the Lord began to lead him, step by step,
into his life work—the teaching of the Word. His first
opportunity came from the Railroad Y.M.C.A. in
Columbia, Pennsylvania, just across the Susquehanna
River from Wrightsville. It was not what might be
called a flattering offer—only a direct request from
Mr. George C. K. Sample, the Secretary of the "Y",
to teach a class of seven or eight railroad men in the
rudiments of spiritual realities. The call had come
unbidden, unsought. There was a need, and he had
been asked to fill it. He dared not disobey the command of the Master whom he had sworn to obey. Perhaps this Master wished to teach His servant, in the
very beginning of his public ministry, that it was not
by might nor by power; that He is altogether able
to take the weak things of the world to confound the
mighty, and that one must learn to be faithful in that
which is least before he can be entrusted with that
which is great. And the servant learned it. During all
his subsequent ministry he never coveted crowds, de-
siring only quality in spiritual service, and knowing
that this could be obtained solely through the unhin-
dered working of the Holy Spirit.

And truly the Spirit wrought in the lives of those

men. An old friend of Mr. McConkey's who watched his work through the years, recently said: "As far as I know, every one of those men became outstanding Christians, and three of them excellent Bible teachers themselves." If it had been our prerogative to assign life work to Christians, we might have said something like this: "Here is a man by nature and training adapted to groups distinctly intellectual; we will place him among college men." But when we look back over the years, we see that He who directs all spiritual placements made no mistake in this case. The men loved him from the first and affectionately called him "Brother Jim." On the other hand, Mr. McConkey's vision was broadened by contacts that were altogether new to him. He was forced to make his teaching plain and practical, though never without that literary finish that delights the inward soul of man whether he be versed in letters or not. Each week he brought to the men the result of his own study; and after the message had been given them orally and their reaction observed, he made whatever alterations were required, and then considered its possibilities for use as a tract. Dozens of his booklets took form in just this way as his work was extended through the years.

The work in Columbia went on from 1891 to 1906, though not regularly through the latter years. Each of the men regarded "Brother Jim" as his spiritual adviser, and often they would go over to his farm, a mile or two south of Wrightsville, where all would sit along the creek bank while they prayed together and talked over their experiences with their common Lord. Mr. George Rost, of Harrisburg, one of the original group, says this: "Eternity alone will ever be able to tell the wonders of his work for his Lord here among men. But this one thing I can say—that from my first meeting with him in 1891 until the day he went home in 1937, a period of 46 years, James McConkey was a true yokefellow with our blessed Lord Jesus Christ. In prosperity or adversity, he was always standing on the platform of explicit faith and trusting in Him who was his Lord and Master."

Eighteen hundred ninety-seven was an important date in the life of James H. McConkey. It was during this year that his first book, *The Threefold Secret of the Holy Spirit*, was published. After the appearance of these articles, in serial form, in a Christian periodical, the need of giving the message a wider and more permanent circulation was pressed upon his heart. He tells us in the following words just how this need was met:

"Its teaching came to me in a time of much suffering and groping after the truth in my earlier Christian life. The light it brought was very precious to my soul, and I longed to pass on the blessing of it to as many others as possible. As I prayed about this, a text was laid heavily upon my heart by the Spirit of God. It was this: 'Freely ye have received; freely give.' I presumed the 'freely' meant 'copiously, aboundingly.' But when I came to look it up, I found, somewhat to my surprise, that it meant 'without price.' Without price ye have received; without price, give. Surely, I thought, the gospel of Jesus Christ is without price received, and without price given. I will put it into God's hands to be given freely to all who desire its message.

"Shortly before, I had met a young Christian business man who was engaged in the free distribution of religious leaflets. I told him what was upon my heart. He said, 'If you give your book to the Lord free, I will give my services free to circulate it.' So, we two Christian laymen struck up a partnership, I to write books, he to print and scatter them. But we had no fund for this. And we realized that the Lord was sending us out without 'purse or scrip,' if we were to go at all. So we began to pray that He would give us some earnest of His will and care in this matter. We had prayed about three weeks when one day there came a letter from a stranger in a distant state. It ran like this: 'These articles have been helpful to me and I wish to help publish them in book form. Enclosed please find twenty-five cents.' That was our 'dew upon the fleece.' It encouraged our faith and intercession so we prayed on. After about two months, there had come from various sources enough funds to issue the first edition of the little book, about one thousand copies. And then began this story. Will you mark its wondrousness? We began to give out the book free to any who requested it. People would write and request it sent to friends and enclose modest offerings to assist in the work. When the thousand books were gone, we found ourselves in possession of a little freewill treasury of ninety dollars. With this we were enabled to publish the second edition of fifteen hundred copies. When these were exhausted, sufficient funds had accumulated from offerings to publish a third edition of three thousand copies. . . . Whenever an edition was exhausted, the Lord had sent enough money to publish the next. Whenever a new book was ready, there was always enough extra money in our treasury to pay for its launching. We never had over-much, nor have we ever had too little." (From *The Sure Shepherd*.)

The Threefold Secret of the Holy Spirit is now in its 430th thousand. More than forty years have passed but its circulation continues on the same plan under the same God.

While Mr. Fred Kelker, of Harrisburg, the Christian business man just mentioned, was busy distributing this message and others that followed in printed form, the author was giving out diligently the new messages just as they were received. Opportunity and extension now came through invitations to teach in other Y.M.C.A.'s—ten classes in a regular route along the Pennsylvania Railroad. One of these was in Coatesville, Pennsylvania, where the local "Y" was being launched. During his first visit there he attended the Iron Rose Bible Class of the Presbyterian church next door, and Mr. William H. Ridgway, the teacher, called on him to speak. In telling of the incident afterwards, Mr. Ridgway said:

"I had about a dozen or so of men in my Iron Rose Bible Class, and Bob Haines, who was helping me in my mission Sunday school at Rock Run, brought Jim into my class. I called on him to speak. This he did, after some urging. I can see him now, tall, slim fellow who wore boots, and when he got up to speak, his pantaloons had slipped up on the boot tops, just like they used to do.

"Jim spoke about the passage where the servant's ear was pinned to the door. Afterwards he became the 'eye-opener' of the Bible Conferences of the Association at Shickelimmy and other points."

After the "Y" in Coatesville became established, Mr. McConkey was called back frequently as a speaker, and always this "tall, gangling fellow," as Mr. Ridgway calls him, was the one to put on the spiritual pressure, to give the devotional tone to every meeting, the one to whom all "Y" men took off their hats. He had no criticism for those who sought to win the ear of the audience by jokes but there was never any place in his message for them. Consecration ran like a golden thread through each, no matter what the subject might be, and levity was out of order—as incongruous as a red tie with a dress suit. Not that he was ever coldly formal but he was always dignified; never solemn but always serious. The yielding of his own life to God, the acceptance of Christ not only as Savior but also as Lord had cost him all he had—his will! In urging others to take the same step, he realized what it would involve, so he could not preface such a challenge with humorous remarks. The Christian life, as he presented it, was the only life of deep, abiding joy, the mere contemplation of which was seriously joyful. Possibly there are Bible teachers who can be facetious without detrimental effect; but James McConkey refused to adulterate his message by unbecoming levity.

During a three days' conference in Coatesville, Pennsylvania, which was held for the purpose of conserving the results of an evangelistic campaign previously launched by Major D. W. Whittle, Mr. McConkey was chosen as one of the speakers and assigned to the Baptist Church. The pastor of that church was the Reverend Benjamin Needham, a black-haired Irishman with a burr in his voice, who listened spellbound to the searching words of the visiting layman. When he had finished, Mr. Needham rose to the pulpit and said, "I don't wish the brither any harm but I just hope the Lord will shut up his business and sind him out to preach the Gospel!"

The ice business, at best, was a dubious venture. There were good years and bad years. Ultimately it proved to be unprofitable, but out of it all the Lord proved to James McConkey that He is the Sure Shepherd who never fails to care for His own. As a result of one of those barren years, he recited this incident which reveals his growing dependence upon the Lord, to Whom he turned with great urgency, even with agony of soul, in years to come.

"Broken health, with its need of an outdoor life, had led me into the wholesale ice business. One winter the ice had come and was ready to cut. I was standing on the river bank directing the operations of my workmen. Suddenly there came a crash; the crunching and grinding of breaking ice, and the cry of 'The ice is going'! The next instant I saw my men fleeing for their lives to the shore. The great field of ice, a mile in width, had broken from its moorings and was rushing down the river. Instantly I realized that a break-up was occurring before my very eyes. At the same moment I overheard one of my men near by saying, 'There goes Mr. McC's bread and butter down the river!' And from the human standpoint that was true, for all my year's business was being swept away at my feet. The bread had ceased; the toil had failed. But almost before the consciousness of what was taking place had laid hold of me there swept into my heart a wondrous sense of peace and quiet as though some strong friend had laid hold to keep me in this sudden moment of test. The messengers who are 'ministering spirits sent forth to minister to the heirs of glory' seemed very close to me that hour. All that day I walked by the river bank amid the wreckage of my year's business, yet seemingly the most unconcerned man upon the scene. I seemed to be conscious of another Man within, keeping in peace the man, who, naturally, would have been torn with disquiet and anxiety. And so there was! And as the year went on God proved to me so beautifully that He could feed me with fish I had not myself caught. In wondrous ways, in ways known only to Himself and me He proved His shepherdship, and taught the sweet lesson that it was eternal and unchangeable even when the ordinary channels through which He had before kept me had failed."

The ice business was not closed out just then, but it became a secondary matter and did not interfere with his teaching activities, opportunities for which increased steadily. His good friends, Mr. Charles L. Huston and Mr. Ridgway, were instrumental in arranging a Y.M.C.A. conference at Sunbury, where Charles E. Hurlbut, W. L. Pettingill, Robert E. Speer, and R. A. Torrey were among the speakers. These men, as well as James McConkey, had not at that time come into prominence. In an old shack outside the hotel, he gave his best; and there, soon after sunrise, was the spiritual emphasis placed on the day. It was this insistence upon the devotional element that gave to this Y.M.C.A. its spiritual foundation.

Other speaking engagements in Pennsylvania followed at the Bloomsburg and Eaglesmere conferences. The story is told of a young man who was importuned by some of his friends to attend a Bible conference. For years he had cultivated the habit of memorizing Scripture every day. He was hungry for more teaching, and to his joy, he found that his soul-hunger could be satisfied by attending the early morning service held by Mr. McConkey, where he simply "ate up" the teaching. At one of the meetings when this man was asked to lead in prayer, all who listened were amazed at the amount of education he had gained from daily, systematic study of the Bible. Mr. McConkey said later in regard to it: "His prayer was a marvel. It was like a rich brocade of silver and gold interwoven with praise, testimony and petition. It was a marvelous thing to hear that young man, a workman in a steel mill, give his testimony for God, and yet it all came from committing one verse of Scripture a day."

As he went to various Y's and summer conferences, he made friends in an unostentatious way with young men who crossed his path. Boating was one of his favorite recreations, and he used even this as an opportunity to become a fisher of men. One of them who often went with him on these excursions enjoys telling how their friendship began. He had sent a telegram to Mr. McConkey and refused to accept pay for it, so a little later Mr. McConkey came around with a pocket Testament for him in which he had written an inscription and signed his name. The men soon learned that he was out to give and not to get, and that the greatest thing he had to give was the Gospel.

Mr. John Riebe of the Moody Bible Institute, in speaking of him at this period of his life, says:

"The men (of the Railroad Y.M.C.A.) loved him and claimed him as one of their number, and such was his influence that it was shared by Christian railroad men throughout the State.

"No less was he appreciated by the college men of the commonwealth. The spontaneity of each group found stimulus from the other as when at conventions, the railroad and college men made the welkin ring with their songs. 'Brother Jim,' as we called him, knew so well how to supply the needed spiritual incentive to call out their devotion."

In speaking of the summer conferences at Shickelimmy (the hotel at Sunbury where the conferences were held), Bloomsburg and Eaglesmere, Mr. Riebe says: "He often found himself the center of a group, giving out in his clear, loving way, the help the hearers needed. In those formative years, teachers like Campbell Morgan, Pierson, Scofield, Torrey, Gray (to mention only a few,) brought 'strong meat' to these gatherings—too strong for some of us, so we could go to Brother Jim with our questions. He would pass the speaker's logic through the prism of his finely trained legal mind, where it would be broken up into component parts until there was nothing left but wonder at the Divine unfolding. It was this rare gift which has made him such a blessing to thousands the world over."

There are Bible teachers who go here and there, deliver their messages, have a few impersonal words with some members of the audience and then proceed upon their way. Not so with Mr. McConkey. He liked to keep on going to the same place, to make friends there, to enter into their interests, pray about their problems and talk informally with small groups concerning things of the Spirit. He began going to Eaglesmere, Pennsylvania, where the first Y.M.C.A. conference was held in the early part of the twentieth century. He continued his visits there until 1930. At this first conference, D. L. Moody was to have been the speaker for the first Sunday evening, but due to a heat stroke, he was unable to leave New York. Mr. McConkey gave the address in his place. This visit was the beginning of a warm personal friendship between him and the Kirk family, who owned the Lakeside hotel there.

Sometime afterward he accepted an invitation to be their guest. On the afternoon of his arrival, as he sat talking with the family about the deep things of God, they were so impressed that they asked others to join them. Guests soon filled the room, seeking the truth as it fell from the lips of this God-illuminated man. From this beginning, he continued to lead the devotional service in the Lakeside Hotel. Each morning he would lay a supply of his tracts on the hotel desk and daily these had to be replaced—a rather remarkable thing for religious tracts in a hotel.

In his gentle, unobtrusive way, he made some lifelong friends at Eaglesmere, among them the Reilys, of Harrisburg. He often went to their tennis court for his exercise, which consisted of a few mild games— never more than half an hour a day. Friends whom he met on the court and in other social ways were soon introduced to his books and tracts. Many of these people became regular supporters of his work. Not that there was ever a word about money! But they were impressed with the messages, and when they saw printed on the back of each a statement to the effect that the work was supported entirely by voluntary offerings, many of them were moved to give.

Most of his systematic teaching at Eaglesmere was done among small groups rather than in regular conferences. The morning devotional hour absorbed most of his energy, but there was another group very dear to his heart—the Boy Scouts employed by the Golf Club as caddies. It was his custom to speak to them on Sunday evenings. Strange did it seem that a man who reached hundreds of thousands through his books should have spoken always to such modest-sized groups, but there were several factors contributing to this. One was the innate modesty of the man, the total absence of any sort of desire to create an effect, to "play to the gallery." Another was his unfavorable physical reaction to a crowd. Perhaps not one out of a thousand of his acquaintances knew this, because his type of nervousness was not easily discernible. Outwardly, he was as placid as a May morning, but there were certain things that bore down upon him with such painful intensity and with such detriment to his whole system that he found it necessary to withdraw when the pressure of the crowd became too great.

Doubtless another reason he did not desire to address large crowds, was the indifference of the masses to his message. They did not want it. Consecration has never been what one might term a popular theme, so he could expect the faithful interest and loyalty of only a moderate number to whom he could speak in a heart-to-heart way, and lead gently into the experience that had been the turning-point of his own life. In this, he was not often disappointed.

III

LENGTHENING CORDS AND STRENGTHENING STAKES

DURING the latter part of the nineteenth century, Mr. McConkey realized that he was designed to be more or less an itinerant. It seemed to be the Lord's will that he should spend his winters in the South—first in North Carolina and Alabama. Wherever he went, there was no lack of calls to teach. About the same time he began to spend the summers in Canada, with the same results. But no matter how far he traveled, there was always the old home in Wrightsville to which he could return. Mrs. Cook, his sister, Margaret, who took over the home after her marriage, had an enviable reputation for good housekeeping, as her mother and sisters had before her. Consequently it was quite a hardship for her to see her brother live chiefly on fruit juices and milk chocolate, while her table was loaded with good things. For several years he was most abstemious in his eating habits. He seldom went to the table, but under pressure, he would avail himself of this privilege when special guests were present. On occasions such as there, his sister would offer her delectable dishes and say, "Jimmie, can't you eat just a little of this?"

And he would reply, "Don't tempt me, Maggie. I feel as if I could eat everything on the table."

The breaking down of the physical had begun before he went abroad in 1884, but all along there had been periods of recuperation and activity followed by occasional periods of nervous indigestion and nerve exhaustion which threatened not only his usefulness but his very life. For this reason he always had to be careful of his diet. An idea of his limited physical strength may be gathered from the fact that *The Threefold Secret of the Holy Spirit* was written in periods of about twenty minutes a day. More time than this spent in writing would inevitably bring on brain-fag, followed by violent headache.

And so he traveled in various parts of the country, a pilgrim, in search of health, spending a good deal of time in Asheville, North Carolina.

During one of his sojourns in that city, the doctor advised horseback riding for him as he was too weak to walk. A work-horse offered by a friend supplied his need and bore him safely across the mountains day by day. On one occasion, he decided to try a new route half-way up the mountain, and on his way came upon a wooden bridge spanning a ravine. He crossed the bridge only to find the road closed on the other side. At this point he noticed the horse seemed to be sick, for its flanks were white with sweat and it was trembling all over, and upon close observation he discovered the bridge was too rotten to attempt recrossing; the horse had sensed this fact before the rider. There was no going forward because the road was closed. The only alternative was to go back, and that was decidedly problematical. The question was whether to lead the animal, drive it, or ride it. The last seemed the answer, so the timid rider mounted the trembling horse again, and fearfully started back. One hind-leg went half-way through the rotten wood of the bridge; but finally the terror-stricken beast reached the other side in safety. That night the rider learned that although there was no barrier before it, the bridge had been condemned for twenty years! But God was just beginning to use James McConkey in earnest; He was not yet ready to take him out of the world!

His visits to North Carolina were responsible for some of his richest friendships. His first meeting with Howard A. Banks was in a hotel in Charlotte, and almost at that moment was formed an amity that ripened into a perfect David-and-Jonathan attachment.

Mr. G. C. Huntington, another of his friends there, tells of how he came to know Mr. McConkey while General Secretary of the Y.M.C.A. (Wherever he went he was sure to seek out the "Y" and was always called upon to speak at meetings among the men.) Sometime in 1902 or 1903 Mr. McConkey asked Mr. Huntington and Mr. Banks to come to his room and pray with him for the healing of his body. Mr. McConkey read James 5: 14-16 and then Mr. Banks anointed him with oil. The three knelt together to ask God that the frail body might be strengthened for service, simply and solely to glorify Him. There was no immediate definite answer but the fact that sufficient strength was granted day by day for about thirty years to carry on a ministry such as very few have ever been privileged to have was proof to Mr. Huntington that the Lord heard and answered that day.

Mr. McConkey did not agree with those who held that healing is in the Atonement in the sense that all one needs to do is to accept it as he accepts salvation— that it is always God's will to heal. His interpretation of that familiar passage, "the prayer of faith shall save the sick," seems logical. It was his conviction, born out of his own experience, that if the believer had unforced, God-given faith that in a particular instance it was God's will to heal, then the patient assuredly would recover. But if the Lord does not send this faith into the soul of the suppliant, he could not work up a faith for healing that would be effective. For more than fifty years, he did not know the meaning of robust health; yet there were special times when he experienced the healing touch of the Lord, the result of which was sufficient strength to carry on the good works for which he had been created in Christ Jesus. He was not opposed to the use of means and frequently consulted doctors, but he believed that there were times when the Lord chose to heal either naturally or miraculously, without the use of medicine. He was not an example of one who had received and continued in perfect health, but he was an example of one who for years had asked for strength sufficient to carry on his God-planned work day by day and had received it.

Naturally, his own experience developed in him the ability to sympathize with and care for others who suffered. Mr. J. K. Coit, whose introduction to him came through Mr. Banks, was staying in the same hotel with Mr. McConkey in Charlotte. In speaking of the time they were together, Mr. Coit says:

"While there I had my first attack of appendicitis, a malady not easily recognized in those days, so I did not know what it was. Brother McConkey nursed me with great tenderness, providing hot water bottles and seeing to it that I stayed in bed. I shall never forget his gracious ministry. . . . During the first year of our married life, and later when we lived in Rock Hill, South Carolina, he was our guest. We have always spoken of those days as a bit of heaven on earth."

About the time he was making these life-long friends in the South, he was also ministering in the North during the summer months, and attracting groups of new friends there. Every summer for a number of years he went to Muskoka, Canada, stopping at the Elgin House, the now famous hotel. Mr. Love, the proprietor, who was a local preacher in the Methodist church, and a very godly man, thought so much of Mr. McConkey that he entertained him from year to year as his guest, insisting upon his having the best room in the house as a token of his appreciation for Mr. McConkey's spiritual influence. It was an unusual hotel, with its conspicuous absence of cards, smoking and drinking. Naturally, such a hostelry would attract none but Christian people; yet it was always full.

Near the hotel was a little chapel in which Mr. McConkey frequently spoke. It was here that he met Canon Fred E. Howitt whose friendship lasted for nearly forty years. Many times afterwards he was invited to speak in Canon Howitt's church (St. George's, of Hamilton, Canada) and gave there his addresses that later formed *The Book of Revelation*. In their home, as elsewhere, he was a welcome guest; Mrs. Howitt and the children enjoyed him as much as the Canon. The family often spoke of three guests who were especially beloved in their home—the Reverend Mr. Luce, of St. Nicholas Church in England, Bishop Taylor Smith, and Mr. McConkey. These three always stood out.

The groups that listened to his messages in Hamilton were not large, but there were always some who already knew and loved his printed messages. Among these was Mr. Dixon, who afterwards succeeded to the rectorship of Trinity Church in Toronto. This man became a prominent figure throughout his diocese because of his good works. He traveled with Moody for a season and later settled in a parish. Wherever the rector went, men marveled at the way God used him, at the secret of his power, not knowing, as Canon Howitt did, that the most revolutionizing force in his life, next to the Bible, had been *The Threefold Secret of the Holy Spirit!*

Canon Howitt, himself, had learned the secret of spiritual power at Keswick, England, before meeting Mr. McConkey, so the two were of one mind. As the years went on, this friendship grew and ripened; the two often spoke in the same meeting in Pittsburgh and other cities. Later, when Mr. McConkey had gone to live in Pittsburgh, the Canon visited him there. As Mr. McConkey had no home in which to entertain his friend, they spent some very happy hours in his office. It was there that he presented his beloved mother (by means of her portrait) and told of her imprint upon his life.

And so it was that these years of his ministry formed a rock foundation for later service. Wherever he traveled, he made spiritual friends without realizing it. Scattered all over the country were those who verily had eaten his messages. They told others, and soon James McConkey came to be in demand as a Bible teacher.

But no matter how wide his field of labor, he never forgot those who had prior claims upon his spiritual interests, those who were his natural responsibilities. Yes, Edwin had fulfilled many of the hopes his elder brother held for him, but he had neglected *the one great thing*.

"Into the life of my dear brother," Mr. McConkey writes, "came this experience. The winter was ending. The ice was breaking in our native river, The freshets were piling it up in great gorges along the banks. A few miles above our home was a little town at which an immense ice gorge had formed in the river. Just below this gorge was an island, upon which the gorge had imprisoned eleven men, women and children. Every one knew the fate which awaited them. The instant this huge ice gorge, with its great weight of water behind it, should break, it would sweep those lives out of existence. My brother learned of the situation. Putting fifty dollars in his pocket, he hastened to the little town. Arriving there, he found the people waiting on the banks of the river for the catastrophe which seemed inevitable. Stepping up to the crowd, he offered fifty dollars to any man who would attempt the rescue of the imperiled ones. But not a man stirred. Again and again did he repeat the offer; but there came no sign of response. Then he sent a little lad into a nearby store for a line. When he brought it out, my brother tied one end of it around his waist, and offered to join with any man who would rope himself to him in an effort to rescue the lives that were

in instant jeopardy of death. Four men roped themselves to the same line of peril with himself, and these
five men, picking their way over the dangerous gorge
at the imminent hazard of their own lives, brought
in safety to the shore every man, woman and child
upon the ice. When my brother offered money to the
people on the river bank, not a man stirred. But when
they saw him give himself and saw the love for these
imperiled lives that was back of it, it drew them to
his side in an instant."

The entire community was thrilled by this exploit
of dauntless daring. Brother James, like everyone else,
admired Edwin's act of unselfish heroism. But for
years the older brother had been thinking of another
life line—the great line of God's love to which he
was hoping and praying that his brother would bind
himself and be saved for time and eternity. So James
McConkey prayed on, speaking a word in season with
all the love and persuasiveness of which he was capable.

Edwin was very reserved about discussing his personal salvation; so their conversations about the matter
were not frequent. But James had made it clear that
he would give the Lord no rest, day or night, until
this prayer was answered. So there could be no doubt
in Edwin's mind as to his brother's position, although
he was not allowed to say a great deal.

Finally, one summer while James was in Canada, he
received a letter from Edwin, who was at Clifton Springs
Sanitarium for treatment, asking him to come. He
went immediately. After his arrival he was told that
Edwin had accepted the Lord Jesus Christ as his Savior.
This joyful news conveyed to him by his sister-in-law

filled his cup of joy to overflowing. Only one Man
could ever say, "The men which thou gavest me . . .
have believed," meaning everyone. But no one was
ever more keenly conscious of his responsibility to his
God-given men than James McConkey. Most of them
"have believed."

Soon after the turn of the century he visited his sister,
Julia, Mrs. John T. Kerr, in Elizabeth, New Jersey.
While there, he had an escape as narrow as the one
in North Carolina. It was in the middle of winter,
and as he was particularly sensitive to the rigors of
the north, it was not surprising that he contracted a
cold. This did not seem alarming until a throat condition developed that became acute. In addition to
this, his tongue became so swollen that he could neither
speak nor swallow. Immediately two of his sisters
were summoned to his bedside. One of them remembered that he had always been able to take country
buttermilk when every other form of food failed. She
sent to Wrightsville for the milk, and when the large
can arrived, it seemed that the problem of nourishment
was solved, for this food had always been taken in
emergencies, and it had never failed. But when the
can was opened, they discovered to their bitter disappointment that it contained nothing but water, all the
buttermilk having been removed! He had believed that
the Lord would use this means for preserving his life,
and now the means had been removed—the Lord alone
remained! The doctor seemed utterly unable to relieve
him, and James McConkey faced one of those crises
in his life which seemed to occur periodically over a
span of years. He wondered if the Lord would come
to the rescue again, for he realized that he could put

no confidence in medical aid at this time. He must cast his burden upon the Lord. He could not voice his own petition, yet he felt the compelling need of mighty intercession. So, raising his weak hand toward heaven, he made known his desire to his brother-in-law, Mr. Kerr, who was a Presbyterian minister. And so it was that the fervent, effectual prayer of this righteous man, combined with that of the sufferer, availed! The restoration was gradual but it was finally completed. It was out of such an experience that he was able to say, "Faith is dependence upon God. And this God-dependence only begins when self-dependence ends. And self-dependence only comes to its end, with some of us, when sorrow, suffering, affliction, broken plans and hopes bring us to that place of self-helplessness where we throw ourselves upon God in seeming utter helplessness and defeat. And only then do we wake to find that we have learned the lesson of faith; to find our tiny craft of life rushing onward to a blessed victory of life and power and service undreamt of in the days of our fleshly strength and self-reliance."

Spending some time on Lake Killarney one summer in Canada, very ill and weak, he was befriended by an old Indian, "Grandfather Roque." Once Mr. McConkey was lying in his little sail-boat, the "Ann," growing weaker every moment under the scorching rays of the sun, yet unable to summon help, for the wind had ceased and the boat could not move. As he lay there, wondering how the Lord would deliver him this time, the Indian came up, lifted him into a row-boat and conveyed him safely to shore. He was so weak after this experience that it was necessary for him to be taken home by one of his sisters—a complete wreck of his former self. So emaciated, so like pictures of the starved in India was he, that his brother could not bear to look at him. This time he could not even digest the buttermilk that had always been his standby when other foods failed!

It was during this illness that Mr. Matthew Kerr, an old friend of the family, intervened. He was the man who had advanced money for the ice-business, whose sons, John and Charles, had married Julia and Blanche McConkey, and who was a fellow-elder in the church. These were his words: "James, I have been praying for you and I believe I have an answer direct from God. It is that I should bring you a bottle of wine which someone gave me some time ago. It has been in my cellar all this while, and I recommend that you take it in milk. I believe your stomach can retain it, and it will help you to get over this spell."

James hesitated. He hated liquor and the liquor traffic. But so did Mr. Kerr. This thing might be from God! So he said simply, "Let's pray about it."

Mr. Kerr knelt by the bed and they both prayed. The result was the full assurance that this was the medicine prescribed by the Lord. He took it and very soon began to grow better.

The friendship between these two continued to be welded until Mr. Kerr's death in 1919. At that time Mr. McConkey wrote to the bereaved family, addressing the letter to his brother-in-law, Mr. Charles M. Kerr:

"Dear Charlie:

"Will you receive for yourself, and convey for me to the girls and John, my tenderest sympathy in the great sorrow that has come to you. Your father's was a beautiful life. Its influence over myself has been felt ever since my boyhood. I thank God for his saintly Christian testimony and the fragrance of his life will linger for years. Uncle Sam, Uncle Henry, and Uncle Matthew were such a trio of God's own as our little church will never see again, and our hearts are full of gratitude that they ever lived in our little home town.

"May the Lord comfort you all, and may your dear father's passing stir us all to more earnest and consecrated living in the realization that we too should 'serve our generation' as he did ere we fall asleep.

"With warmest love to all,

"Affectionately,
"Brother Jim"

IV

OTHER SHEEP

It was inevitable that a man who had come into so much spiritual light should be led into various ways of dispensing that light. So, we find James McConkey, along with Fred Kelker, Charles Hurlbut, and George Sample, among those who were back of Peter Cameron Scott in the founding of the Africa Inland Mission. Mr. McConkey's most definite service to the Mission began in 1903 when he gave much of his time to deputation work. The January-February (1904) issue of *Hearing and Doing*, the organ of the Mission, gives the following news item:

"Mr. James H. McConkey has taken up work in several New Jersey towns and expects to teach in that State and in New York during the rest of the winter months, returning to the Lake cities in the early spring. While our brother devotes most of his time to Bible teaching, in his meetings at each place he arranges to give at least one lantern address on the work of the Africa Inland Mission. Shall we not remember him constantly in prayer as he gives out these messages on the Word and the work?"

Mr. McConkey had founded *Hearing and Doing* and was the active editor of this periodical for eight or ten years, after which he remained a contributing editor, while Howard A. Banks and J. D. Adams were editors. It is interesting to see how he gave his *best* in each issue—there were never any shortcuts. Unless he had a message fresh from God, he wrote nothing. So, in the April-June (1906) issue, we find the following jottings from his pen which have not appeared elsewhere:

"The grace of God, which suffers so patiently the coldness of His children, seems almost more amazing than that same grace which bears with the rebelliousness of sinners. For those have known the depths of a love which these have never tasted."

* * *

"God never has designed, and never will endure, any substitute for the individual, consecrated, Spirit-filled believer. And any church which falls short of being a company of such is, in His sight, a dismal failure, however elaborate its organization."

* * *

"One of the greatest rivers in Europe, with all its abundance of life-giving waters, rises in the very heart of an Alpine glacier. God, by the power of His Spirit, can cause the coldest heart to burst forth in streams of divine love and blessing."

* * *

"Here is a bit of prayer for your morning watch, child of God: 'All through this day, O Lord, let me touch as many lives as possible for Thee. And, every life I touch, do Thou by Thy Spirit quicken, whether through the word I speak, the prayer I breathe, or the life I live.' "

"Some men are full of grace. And some are full of truth. Jesus was 'full of grace *and* truth.' So God's call to us is to 'speak the truth in love.' To speak to men in love without truth—that is weakness. To speak to men the truth without love—that is harshness. He alone is in God's perfect will who does both, even as Jesus did. Yet let it be remembered that God may bless grace without truth, because of the very grace that is there. And He may bless the truth, too, without grace, because of the truth which is there. Yet in so doing, He does not seal the lack of truth in the one case, nor the lack of grace in the other. Nay, but it means that since He cannot have perfect instruments, He seals with His Spirit whatever is true and gracious in the imperfect and incomplete. So should we indorse the truth wherever given, even while we deprecate any lack of love in the giving. So also we should stand against error, whoever teaches it; yet we should deal in love with the man so teaching."

* * *

"God gives us vision as a stimulus to service. God gives service as a balance-wheel to vision. When there is no vision, service wanes. When service is neglected, vision fades. Communion without service will end in sentiment. Service without communion will soon become drudgery. 'We will give ourselves to prayer and ministry,' said the apostles. They went from prayer to ministry, and then from ministry back to prayer. Yoke these two together and you have spiritual symmetry. Divorce them and you have spiritual lopsidedness. Either, without the other, makes us like a boat with but one oar, a bird with but one wing. We do not progress. We only turn round and round in a circle of spiritual emotionalism, or round of monotonous drudgery."

*   *   *

"The man who is going about to establish his own righteousness will have but a poor establishment when it is done. It will stand the test of neither fire, thieves, nor time. The only flame-proof, burglar-proof, eternity-proof righteousness is the 'righteousness of God,' which is by faith alone."

*   *   *

" 'All things are possible to him that believeth.' 'He could do there no mighty works because of their unbelief.' There is nothing God *cannot* do for the man who *trusts*. There is nothing God *can* do for the man who *distrusts*."

*   *   *

"The place to meet sin is at the gateway of the imagination. Shut it out at that point, and you will live a life of continuous victory. But let it in there, and you have a traitor within who will rise up and betray you to your ruin at any moment. Guard the outpost of your mind with unceasing watchfulness, and the foe will never carry the inner citadel of the will. The foul desire, the enslaved will, the impure act—all begin with the polluted imagination. They are but the three successive acts in the tragedy of the soul's downfall—a tragedy which would never have had a beginning if the portals of the thoughts had been steadfastly sealed against the enemy."

*   *   *

"You men and women who are really *heart-hungry for power, remember this: We dim the light and mar the power of the Spirit of God within us every time we yield our members to the doing of anything which He Himself would not do if He were living in this body of ours.*

"But that is just where He is living. And so we dim the forth-shining of His light and check the forth-flowing of His power when we do these things. Now it is not for us, nor any other man or woman, to tell you what these are. But if you will lay this axiom down on one side of your life, and lay God's Book down on the other, it will not take you long to see for yourself. And that very seeing is the first needful step toward the signal victory which is going to be yours when, in the power of the Spirit, you begin to *live* as you *see*."

* * *

"And as to this matter of being too busy to pray, it comes to this: We are never too busy to do that which we deem to be of supreme importance. We always find time for that. So then, is it not through our belittling the importance of prayer that we fail to find time for it? If the opportunity does not come along in the natural course of events—if you do not seem to *have* it, then *make* it. How do you manage to discuss matters of great moment with men? If you do not have the time, you *make an engagement. Make an engagement with God.* And then *keep* it. You would not think of breaking troth with men. Then do not break tryst with God, either. Keep your appointment to meet Him in the secret place at least as sacredly as you would to meet your best human friend."

———

In the same issue, the following editorial appeared:

"Our beloved brother, Mr. James H. McConkey, after a season of rest at home, has been teaching in

Olean, New York, and is at this writing having service in Erie, Pennsylvania. From this point, he expects to go to Canada, where he will probably spend the summer. We are indeed glad and grateful for his slowly returning health and feel sure our readers will continue to remember him in prayer. The *Jottings* which we publish in this issue are the latest and richest we have had from his pen."

Later, in the year 1906, an article appeared under the caption of "Christ, Our Sin-Bearer." A large part of this article was later published in tract form under the caption of *God's Jewel Case*. During the years 1906, '07 and '08, *Hearing and Doing* carried as first articles, "Jacob's Struggle," "Safety," "Give God a Chance," and "Believing is Seeing," all of which were later published in tract form.

It was while he was editor of *Hearing and Doing* that Mr. McConkey coined the phrase, "As to needs, full information; as to funds, no solicitation," and he carried this principle into all the Christian work with which he was later connected. There were two things that marked the branches of Christian work to which he gave his vital interest, and they were inter-denominationalism and voluntary support. He did not spend time in deploring the weaknesses of the denominational organizations, nor their methods of obtaining money, but he quietly invested his time and influence in Bible teaching among various denominations, in Bible schools, in faith missions and in tract distribution, supported voluntarily by various denominations. Until recently we had never seen expressed in words the sentiment just quoted from *Hearing and Doing*: "We should stand against error, whoever teaches it;

yet we should deal in love with the man so teaching."
We had seen that conviction lived out in his life. While
he did not spend time in dealing with negatives, one
always knew where to find him. There was never a
shadow of doubt as to his position in regard to anything akin to error in doctrine; but on the other hand
there was never any lack of charity toward the offender
who had erred from the truth. Those who listened
were magically drawn to his words because of the marvelous balance of grace and truth they exhibited. One
did not have to listen to a tirade on Modernists before
he could get a grain of constructive teaching, but one
never heard an address by him without realizing that
he was diametrically opposed to Modernism. Thus did
he practice what he preached!

Sometime before his activities in the Africa Inland
Mission, he was connected with another faith work that
had a far-reaching outlook but which has since gone
out of existence. This was the Pennsylvania Bible Institute in Philadelphia. This school, which was founded
in 1895, had no official connection with either of the
Bible schools now in Philadelphia, but Mr. Rugh, who
later founded the Bible Institute of Pennsylvania, was
one of its graduates, and Dr. Pettingill, who founded
the Philadelphia School of the Bible, was at one time
a member of its faculty. Nor was there any official connection between the Pennsylvania Bible Institute and the
Africa Inland Mission, but some of the same men were
vitally interested in both. Prior to the founding of
the school, Mr. Charles E. Hurlbut, who later became
the Director of the mission, planned a canvass of all
West Philadelphia west of Fiftieth Street, north and
south, for the purpose of evangelizing it and estab-

lishing a training school there. And who was better
fitted to train the personal workers than his friend,
James McConkey? So he was called, and he came to
conduct this class—to bring out the precious truths he
had learned about consecration, prayer, and the premillennial coming of the Lord.

It was in one of the classrooms of this Bible school
a few years later, he met his old friend, Henry Frost,
whom he had not seen since college days. Dr. Frost
went into the room where several men were gathered,
and one of them whom he did not recognize strode
toward him, threw his arms around him, put his head
on his shoulder and wept. There was a moment of
embarrassment for Dr. Frost could not think who it
might be. Time and illness had taken such heavy toll
that the friend of years ago was not easily recogniz-
able. But that rich, peculiar quality in the voice
established James McConkey's identity. Then there
was more embracing and also more tears. These close
friends were always "James" and "Henry" to each
other—never "Jim" and "Harry" or "Jack," as they
were called by other Princeton boys, and their union
was not affected by absence. In fact they did not see
each other again for a number of years—once at a
Conference at Muskoka, and again at a Conference
in Pittsburgh where they were both on the program.
But, as Dr. Frost afterward said, they did not need
to see each other or to write. Their friendship was
fixed; indeed it was eternal. And during the rest of
his life, Mr. McConkey, although he was not connected
officially with the China Inland Mission of which Dr.
Frost was Director, gave this work his whole-hearted
support.

V

FRIENDSHIPS IN PITTSBURGH

VARIOUS factors contributed to a removal from Wrightsville as a base, and Mr. McConkey felt definitely led in 1914 to make his home in Pittsburgh. It was perfectly natural that he should seek out a Y.M.C.A. as soon as he arrived there. His experience had been largely in the Association. Living was inexpensive there, but best of all, it afforded him wider contacts with men. He was distinctly a man's man, and it was among them that he did most of his spiritual work; so he began his ministry in this city by speaking at the Friday lunch-hour in the Central "Y". The International Sunday School Lesson was the topic.

In the fall of 1915, he went to the East Liberty "Y" to live and made this his headquarters as long as he was in Pittsburgh. Mr. Bard McCandless, who was rooming there at the time, tells of his surprise when Mr. McConkey, after saying, "Let me feel your racket," borrowed it, and then played an excellent game of tennis, explaining afterwards that he had been a semi-invalid for years and could not play more than two sets at a time. He entered into it with great zest, however, despite the handicap of not having played his first game until after his fiftieth birthday. He was a skilled player, thinking through every stroke. Small wonder for he used his head in everything. It was not long before he and Mr. McCandless were challenging any combination that came along. Competitive games of this character enabled him to make contacts with men that eventually proved to be the basis of lasting friendships. When those men of the "Y" went to their rooms, they began to talk of this new friend that had come into their lives—how he lifted the level of their conversation by raising it from the commonplace interests of daily life to spiritual realities.

The old court plot which was afterwards sold for eight hundred thousand dollars is now a part of the grounds of the University of Pittsburgh. It was here that Mr. McConkey watched the tennis tournaments, studying meanwhile the grip and stroke of champions. For years afterwards, as long as he had strength for outdoor exercise, he played tennis. Even when playing was forbidden, his interest in the game continued. He scanned every paper for news. It gave the physical man a much needed recreation, but this was not all. James McConkey was the calculating type. If he had been a man of the world, he would have calculated in terms of his business or profession, but since he was a man of God, he calculated in terms of heaven. Whether he ate or drank or played games it was with reference to God. How similar his method was to Saint Paul's—"For though I be free from all men, yet have I made myself servant unto all, that I may gain the more. And unto the Jews I became as a Jew that I might gain the Jews; to them that are under the law as under the law, that I might gain them that are under the law—To the weak became I as weak that I might gain the weak; I am made all things to all men that I might by all means save some." So it was that skill in tennis as in other things was turned to account in Christian service. James McConkey, like the Apostle to the Gentiles, was a spiritual calculator. Obviously, tennis was not an end in itself, but it did afford opportunity for him to meet men on their own ground and to establish friendly intercourse. It was a wedge to open an avenue to the soul that spiritual truth might enter and find a congenial habitation.

He was a close student of psychology; he studied the minds of the men on the court so he might the better understand them in the dormitory. Never did a salesman study his customers with keener scrutiny, never was a politician more alert to win supporters than was Mr. McConkey to lead men in paths of righteousness and truth. While few of them ever took the trouble to analyze the situation, they intuitively knew that this friend of theirs was actuated by the highest and purest motives—he was really interested in them, in their present and future welfare, in revealing to them the life that is hid with Christ in God. One very simple rule of psychology he always applied was his habit of addressing individuals by their names instead of saying "you," or apologizing for failure to remember names. He never forgot a face. Frequently the names of old acquaintances would slip from his mind. As he sat in the lobby of the "Y" quietly meditating, some man he knew would appear. Immediately he would slip over to one of his dormitory friends, get the name straight, then hurry back to the man in question, calling him by name. This little trick of psychology always worked. After the ice was broken he could soon guide the conversation, without embarrassment, into the realm of the spiritual. However, he did not always follow this method, for he believed that speech should be *seasoned* with salt—not *be* salt!

It was at the East Liberty "Y" that he received his D.D. degree, for there he was dubbed "Dean of the Dormitory." A unique position this—a self-appointed, self-supporting, spiritual adviser, moving so quietly among them that few realized what a reservoir of spiritual power was in their midst. But it was just the kind of job he liked, one that involved no responsibility to human authority and depended on no human group for maintenance. I think "voluntary" was one of his favorite words; I can hear him say it now; and I believe he loved the personal, evangelistic work there primarily because it was voluntary. He prayed for openings, and when the time came to act, the Spirit led, the Spirit empowered, the Spirit brought the work to fulfillment. Many times he talked with men in a corner of the lobby, at other times in his quiet little room on the fourth floor, but wherever it was, men felt first of all his personal interest in them—an interest devoid of any possible selfish end. Then it was that they came to realize that underneath, above, and beyond it was the all-absorbing desire for the glory of his Lord. Why did they give such earnest and reverent attention to his words? It was because they realized that this man with all the quiet intensity of his nature was daily and hourly obeying the great commandment given by our Lord: "Freely ye have received, freely give."

It is impossible to estimate the volume of spiritual power that went out from these walls, and perhaps we should not attempt to make spiritual estimates. Every now and then some business man witnesses to the way this servant of the Most High was used in his life during such contacts as these, but until that day when every man's work shall be made manifest, when it shall be revealed whether he has built* upon the one foundation, gold, silver, precious stones, wood, hay or stubble, we shall not be able to determine the value thereof.

Nor was the public ministry neglected. At that time the Pittsburgh district was unique because there were approximately one hundred big business men in that great industrial center who were outstanding Christians. A number of these men recognized Mr. McConkey's teaching gift and made frequent demands on him to address their meetings. Sometimes the services were held in churches of various denominations, but usually these inter-denominational gatherings were in other public buildings. He always operated according to fundamental spiritual principles. He aimed to strengthen the churches by strengthening whatever individual members he could reach with the spiritual food he had to offer. Pastors never objected to him because they knew he was not trying to start a movement or organize a group outside the church, but unfortunately few of them realized their debt to this man who had revitalized the spiritual life of some of their most influential members. Men and women who sat at his feet heard about consecration, saw it exhibited in human life, breathed it in the very air, and went back to their churches spiritually quickened. His accurate knowledge of the Word and a natural logical quality of mind made

* See I Cor. 3:12.

an excellent background for a teacher; but if this had been all, James McConkey would have been in a class with hundreds of other Bible teachers, and his name would be sinking fast into oblivion even now. No, these qualities, valuable as they are, do not make the heart burn. How often have we heard him say, "Watch for the burning heart when you read your Bible!" Those who listened to him unfold the Word felt the burning heart and, beyond doubt, this work of the Spirit was done because the instrument was yielded, because he himself had presented his body a living sacrifice. It was not hard for men to believe that "when the burnt offering was laid on the altar, then the song of the Lord began." Before their very eyes was one who had laid his all on the altar and in whose heart the song *had* begun.

While James H. McConkey is known throughout Christendom and in the evangelized areas of heathen countries by his books and tracts, it is in Pittsburgh perhaps, as in no other place, that he is most widely known in a personal way. There, when his name is mentioned, the minds of scores of men of affairs turn first of all to his personality rather than to his productions. One of the first friends he made after going to Pittsburgh to live was Dr. Thomas A. Miller, who has told us something of his first impressions in the following words published in the November (1937) issue of *Christ Life* magazine:

"Mr. McConkey impressed me during those early years (1914-18) with his poise, intelligence, and serene aspect. His manner was simple, gracious, but dignified, and perhaps somewhat reserved. His speech was, as I recall, characterized by a certain deliberation or reticence; his voice quiet, soft, well-modulated, and pleasing. In conversing, he usually inquired with old-fashioned courtesy, and apparent interest concerning your family, yourself, common friends, and so forth. He was warm-hearted and would not infrequently assure one of his friendship and regard. He possessed in health a kindly, sparkling intelligent eye, and a ready, attractive smile.

"He impressed you as one who knew and walked with God, living much in the secret place of the Most High. There was about him that indefinable something suggestive of the mystic, the recluse, and the prayer closet.

"Mr. McConkey possessed a cultivated, intelligent, logical, finely organized mind. Lucidity, directness, sanity, brevity of diction and expression, a sweet reasonableness and persuasiveness, together with warmth, and an absence of rhetorical flourish or emotional display or extravagance characterized his writings. . . .

"He was not carried away by vagaries or extravagances or false emphases. He was rooted and grounded in the Word and had a remarkably clear view of the truth as it is in Christ Jesus and set forth in His Word. He was a safe, sane, gifted expositor and guide into the secret things of God."

His teaching ministry in Pittsburgh and elsewhere was not denominationally bound, nor was it limited to churches. Some of his most fruitful work was among the personnel of big business firms, as well as in the Y.M.C.A., and other laymen's groups scattered over the city. Those who accepted the teaching went back to their churches strengthened and more efficient than before. At McCann's, one of the largest retail food stores in America, he began with small prayer-meetings confined principally to the managers. Mr. Walter P. Fraser, who was president at that time, and other officials of the firm were warm, personal friends and men whose hearts the Lord had touched by means of this servant of His. Luncheon meetings were held four days in the week at which Mr. McConkey often spoke, but whether or not he was present, they knew he was upholding them in prayer, knew that any petition brought to him would be faithfully carried to the Lord until the answer came. He was free to go in and out of the store as he pleased. Well did the most humble employee know that this tall figure moving so quietly among them had an indefinable something, a beautiful intimacy with the Lord of life that few could claim or prove.

In most cases, his books had preceded him in the lives of these friends, and they had begun to love the man through his message. His books and pamphlets held a sacred place in their hearts, as did the place in which they were penned. On one occasion when Mr. Fraser was visiting Mr. McConkey in Wrightsville, Pennsylvania, it happened that the two were walking together in the yard of the old home. Mr. McConkey pointed to the "upper room" in which *The Threefold Secret of the Holy Spirit* had been written, and said, "There's the place where the Lord gave me my first message." And Mr. Fraser bared his head!

The prayer he prayed for these friends was much like that of Paul in Colossians 1: 9-11. In addition to this, the Lord granted material blessing to them and caused their business to prosper. If any were sick, he not only visited them but held on in prayer until

the will of the Lord was made clear. But perhaps the
attribute of his character that appealed most to the
men and women in that part of the work-a-day world
was his sameness; never worried, never impatient,
never in doubt. They always knew where to find him.
After a request had been made to God, with prayer
and thanksgiving, there was no cause to be anxious.
His audible prayers were very simple and direct and
apparently with little effort. There was no physical
agonizing, but just a statement of the need followed
by expressions of confidence in the One who had
promised to supply all need.

In visiting friends in business he often gave them,
in the course of conversation, a Scripture text appli-
cable to the problems that were most pressing just at
that moment. Mr. Clark M. Kefover, who was one of
his most intimate friends, remarked that if friends
asked for advice, he gave it, and it was always sound.
He had unusual judgment in business matters. Thus,
it was by this personal interest in the business and
home affairs of his friends that Mr. McConkey made
a sure pathway to their hearts.

But this was not all. In an informal way he was
teaching men and women how to interpret and apply
the truths of Scripture. He was training them for
wider stewardship. In doing this, the conspicuous element in his method was that he did not have the usual
attitude of the professional teacher. He was simply
a comrade, a yokefellow with even the youngest of
Christians. No matter how untaught one might be, in
this man's presence, he was not uncomfortable.

There was one command, however, that he did not
obey and that was, "Reprove, rebuke . . ." unless one

might interpret an eloquent silence on certain occasions as a reproof, a rebuke! Perhaps that was it, and many who were slow to interpret went on their way unwittingly. But usually he had positive words of encouragement like those he gave a Christian business man who came to him much discouraged because an employee, whom he had been trying to lead to the Lord, showed no sign of response. Moreover, a business associate, also a Christian, had rebuked him about the matter and exhorted him to more zeal! But not so "Brother James"! He simply said, "C——, you have no cause to worry about that. You have been faithful in praying for this fellow and in showing him the Way of life. The Lord does not hold us responsible for results."

In another city a young woman having more zeal than knowledge was taken to task by a young man when she spoke of Mr. McConkey's books being like leaven. "Why, don't you know," he said, "that in Scripture leaven is always a type of evil? That parable doesn't teach that the whole world will be converted gradually. You will see that in the Scofield Reference Bible. I suppose, of course, you have one?" The truth was that she had never heard of the Scofield Bible; and, while Mr. McConkey himself regarded Dr. Scofield's notes highly, in all their association he had never suggested that she get one. He had been too intent on encouraging her to risk very many suggestions—or corrections! Perhaps he knew there would be others who delighted in giving both.

In Pittsburgh, Miss Georgina Negley had been another of the timid ones, but he had gently influenced her to take an executive position in a Christian woman's organization which afterwards became a means of widespread evangelistic work in hospitals and other institutions in the city.

Doubtless his friends regarded humility as his outstanding virtue, but it was a humility entirely unconscious of itself. He had a way of classing himself with ordinary Christians, that made one feel that he almost belonged there. He never spoke of being humble, or spent any time in self-deprecatory remarks, but simply took his place in company with the mediocre type of Christians and walked as a true yokefellow, always bearing the heavier part of the load. He did not pride himself on any peculiarities and made no effort whatever to be distinct from his fellows, unless it was a uniqueness in spiritual devotion. There was no mark of genius on the outward man—only the mark of suffering left by early years which even the inner radiance of the soul had not completely destroyed. His friends were chosen from every round of the social ladder, but no one would ever infer from any act, or word, or inflection of the voice, that he recognized any social differences among them. They had a common Father. That was enough.

The Christian Life Conferences that began in Pittsburgh in 1915 made good use of Mr. McConkey and his printed messages. These meetings held on Friday, Saturday and Sunday in various churches went on throughout the year except the summer months—usually about forty of them each year. He felt that his ministry was especially to Christians—to give the truth that would help most in deepening their spiritual lives. Those who sat at his feet did not go to hear a discussion of international problems, or a discourse on social service or what-not. What they wanted was an intimacy with the One who had redeemed them, a closeness which this man seemed to know as few others did. And so they listened with open heart as he talked of surrender and prayer and the Holy Spirit.

Excruciating headaches placed severe limitations on Mr. McConkey's work. Not more than twenty or thirty minutes of concentration a day was possible without periods of relaxation. He might have become more or less of a recluse if necessity had not forced him away from study and writing. These intervals of rest were opportunities for contacts. Much of his time was used in simple visiting, in getting close to the hearts of the people in their homes. He heard their problems and prayed through with them. When he told a man, "I am praying about that matter," the man knew he would be questioned later as to whether the answer had come, and would continue to be questioned until it did come. Doubtless he himself was constrained to pray as he never would have prayed otherwise.

Mr. John E. Nelson, of Pittsburgh, tells how Mr. McConkey won the hearts of his children by entering into their interests as if he had been of their generation. They were always delighted to have him come. One night as soon as he opened the door, the little girl called out to her brothers, "Oh, Billy McConkey is here!" He cherished the love of children so much that he enjoyed repeating this left-handed compliment.

One night the Nelson family had quite a surprise when he said to one of the children who had been taking violin lessons, "Let me see your violin." Thereupon he tuned it, tucked it under his chin, and played as they seldom had heard an amateur play. But when he laid it down, he said, "I had to give that up. It took too much out of me—haven't touched a violin for six years."

Miss Edith Nelson, though she was enriched by the printed messages and the oral ones given before her church group, said it was as a friend, primarily, that she loved to remember "Brother James"—his tender solicitude for all the family, his appreciation of every small service, and his keen interest in her small affairs, even to her winning out in tennis against a young man from the "Y".

He was always eager to get the reaction of real friends to his messages. One night in the course of an address he told a story about a Scotchman who said to his wife, "Mary, when I get to glory, I'll be so taken with looking at the Savior's face, I don't expect to see you for the first hundred years." As he returned home with the young couple who had taken him to the appointment, and talked with them about various points in the message, the young lady said, "I couldn't help but feel sorry for Mary, if her husband was not to see her for a hundred years!" Mr. McConkey seemed a little surprised at this reaction and said, "Oh, did it affect you that way? Perhaps I had better use some other illustration." And he did.

VI

BIRTH OF THE SILVER PUBLISHING SOCIETY

THE period from 1915 to 1930 was without doubt the most fruitful of Mr. McConkey's life. The hidden ministry in and around Pittsburgh for nine months in the year, the teaching ministry in Georgia, Alabama, and Virginia during the winter months, and most of all, the wide extension of the printed-page ministry, bear us out in this conviction. As soon as he became settled in Pittsburgh, he began to pray that the Lord would open the way for him to establish an office from which to disseminate his books and tracts. The appeals for his messages were steadily growing in number. To supply the demand he must have adequate accommodations. Mr. Kelker continued to lend valuable assistance from his headquarters in Harrisburg, but Mr. McConkey had a firm conviction that the time had come for him to branch out for himself, to establish an office where he could give exclusive supervision to the circulation of his books and tracts. This plan would not supersede Mr. Kelker's activities, but rather supplement them. He shared this dream with Mr. Bard McCandless, a young Christian who had not yet had the vision of "praying down money" and who said right off, "I think that's fine, Mr. McConkey. Now I can tell you of several wealthy women whom you can

75

approach, and no doubt some of them will provide the money you need."

"No," he replied decidedly, "I will never do that, and you must not do it for me. I will never ask men for money with which to carry on God's work. If He wants this thing done He will touch the heart of the one who should give it. Let's just keep praying that He will send a man who will offer five thousand dollars. If He does this, we'll know it's His seal on the work."

After praying for about a year and a half, he sought out his friend one day and announced joyfully, "McCandless, I believe I've met the man. Just as I was leaving the Duquesne Club today where I had given a message, Mr. ———— came to me and said, 'I have been thinking about the circulation of your books and wondering if you could use a little money for it.' I told him I could and was wondering what he meant by 'a little money' when he said, 'Would five thousand dollars be enough?' "

Mr. ———— was just leaving for a two months' vacation, but as soon as he came back the cash was turned over, an office rented, and the larger book-and-tract distribution was begun under the name of the Silver Publishing Company. ("Company" was changed to "Society" when the organization was incorporated in 1922.) This name was chosen in memory of his beloved mother, Susan Ruth Silver. In the course of time Mr. ———— donated eighty thousand dollars to the work, and shortly before his death he remarked that he had never regretted a single dollar.

From the very first, the Silver Publishing Society had the simple financial policy of "No soliciting. No debt." As the books were sent out on a wider scale, and as the work became better known, the voluntary offerings increased, and at the end of each year there was a small balance. No matter how pressing the office needs became, no debt was incurred, but more prayer was offered! And always the Lord supplied the need just on time. The office at 1013 Bessemer Building became known around the world both as a dispensary for free literature and a place where prayer was wont to be made. Every day the little office force laid aside their work and took their own needs and the petitions that had come in letters and spread them before the Lord. This was one of the secrets of steady and continual blessing on the work.

The plan of office procedure was simply to send the McConkey books and tracts free to anyone, anywhere, who would request them. He reasoned that if one "reached after it" by writing a letter or postal card, the message would be read when it was received. Advertisements to this effect were placed in Christian periodicals; responses came, orders were filled, and the work grew steadily. There was never any mushroom growth. The founder always had a horror of this. No mention was ever made of money except the simple statement printed on the back of each book: "The work is supported by voluntary offerings." He believed that if people were blessed by the messages, and knew that the work was dependent on free-will offerings, they would give as the Lord enabled them. Knowing that some could give more, others less, and still others nothing at all, he did not wish the third class to be deprived of the privilege of reading the books, and so the offer was to *all*. He had no criticism of Christian authors who sold their books in the usual way through publishers, but he had a strong conviction that this was not God's way for him. He had set His seal on the plan as it had been used by Mr. Kelker. Was not this reason enough to continue it? There was one difference in the methods of the two men. Mr. Kelker sent a book only when it was requested by the individual; Mr. McConkey sent books requested by one individual for another, or a number of books requested for a group. This new project did not hinder Mr. Kelker's work at all. It was the divinely appointed plan for giving a much wider circulation to the messages than they would have had otherwise.

During that first year (1917) many "blessing letters," as he called them, came to encourage Mr. McConkey's heart. Extracts from a few are quoted below:

———

"Erie, Pa.

"At a recent meeting of our Ministerial Association, the president of that organization made the statement that McConkey's *The Threefold Secret of the Holy Spirit* had been of inestimable value to both himself and some of his friends.

"He suggested that we get in touch with you, and that we have this book sent to every one of our pastors. In accordance with this request, will you kindly forward at your earliest convenience fifty copies and advise me the cost of these books, in order that I may make proper remuneration? I understand that Mr. McConkey's books are published entirely through voluntary offerings, and that no charge is made for their distribution. In this matter, however, we wish to make a contribution commensurate with the cost of the books, and request that you advise us in this."

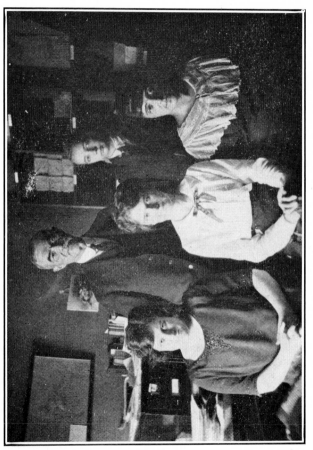

Mr. McConkey and his office force, Pittsburgh, Pa.

The McConkey Home, Wrightsville, Pa., before it was remodeled

"Grand Rapids, Mich.

"Will you please send me *The Threefold Secret of the Holy Spirit, Prayer,* and *The Surrendered Life?* I would also like to have the ten leaflets mentioned in the back of the last-named book.

"Several years ago, I wrote Fred Kelker for *The Surrendered Life,* but under the guiding hand of God he sent *Prayer.* It resulted in six months of such prayer as I never knew before, in the saving of my home from being broken up, and God's showing me I was to blame. But Jesus removed the cause, and we are happy in the wonderful things God has done for us. Both *The Threefold Secret* and *Prayer* have been passed on, and my wife has asked for them again."

"Memphis, Tenn.

"Will you please send me a copy of the book, *Prayer?* God alone knows what a change the reading of the two preceding books has wrought in my life, and I firmly believe God has spoken to me through the last one, *The Surrendered Life,* and has shown me what my life work is to be."

"Huntington Park, Calif.

"I received the copy of *The Threefold Secret of the Holy Spirit,* and one for a preacher-friend. I had an old copy given me seventeen years ago (1900). The book clarifies that much misunderstood subject more than any one writing I ever saw; and my sermon on the subject was a revelation to many good people. I thank you more than I can tell you."

"Edmeston, N. Y.

"The little book, *The Threefold Secret of the Holy Spirit*, came to me last evening, and I think the receipt of it was Divinely timed. Owing to severe stomach trouble, I am laid aside from my work for a time, and as I could not be at my services this beautiful Easter day, I have read the book through. I can hardly tell you how much I have enjoyed it. It is much along the line of my beliefs and teaching. I am fearing, however, that I have taught the truths better than I have lived them. I think the book will enrich both my life and my teaching.

"I wish all our young theological students could read it to get the benefit of it early in their ministry. I am sending you $1.00 to help in its distribution."

———

Such letters were Mr. McConkey's pay-envelopes, the only ones he ever received from the Silver Publishing Society. He contended that salaries equivalent to the wages paid elsewhere for similar work should be paid those in his office, but he would never accept one cent of salary for himself. His own living was provided by the Lord in other ways. There are some things, as we all realize, that are too precious to be appraised— a patriot could not be paid for giving his life to his country, a good mother could not set a price on her service to her child; no amount of money could compensate a man for giving his all! Of course no real mother would ever want pay for bringing up her child, and a man who loved enough to give his all would not desire remuneration. Just so with James McConkey. The messages themselves had cost his all. They would never have been fraught with power such as they were, if the author had not first presented his body a living sacrifice; so, dispensing with a salary was a small matter compared with his early struggle to surrender the will. Perhaps he had been influenced by Hudson Taylor and the China Inland Mission in this, even before the founding of the Africa Inland Mission, and had seen the effect of first obeying the Lord's command to preach the Gospel and then trusting Him to supply all needs. Whatever the explanation might be, nothing could induce him to accept any part of the offerings received for his personal use. "Faith" work was comparatively new in those days, and some of the great faith missions were not recognized by leaders in denominational organizations. One of these denominational men approached Mr. McConkey one day and said, "Look here, you are handling a lot of money, it seems. What Board are you under? To whom do you make your reports?"

To this he quietly replied, "We are under the Lord, and I make my reports to Him."

"I know, but you ought to report to some Board."

"Well," he replied again, "I call my constituency together at frequent intervals and tell the amount of our offering and something of the way the money is used. We send out a report to our larger constituency, which gives all the important facts concerning our finances."

So the man went away half satisfied.

The report giving the amount of the offerings and the items of expense was sent once a year to contributors to the work. A card index file listing the amount and date of the offering was kept in the office. At the end of each year there was a small balance, and no debt. One of the constituents, a big business man, once remarked to Mr. McConkey, "I see from the report that your balance at the beginning of the year was $5.25, and you handled $20,000 during the year. Show me a business firm in Pittsburgh that can do a $20,000 business on $5.25!"

One may close his eyes and see something of the network that was being formed not only in this country but in other lands. Christians, who, aforetime, had seen no personal work they could do, now began to enclose the McConkey tracts in letters, to give them out in meetings, to use them in Sunday school classes and missionary societies, to keep them on hand for any emergency that might arise. The advertising went on as funds permitted, and in 1922 alone there were fifteen thousand answers. Many of those who received free literature never contributed anything. Others have given at regular intervals up to the present time.

During those early years the work in the office was done by a young man (a husky Swede), Miss Winifred McDonald, who was the office secretary, and Mr. McConkey himself, with most of it falling on Miss McDonald. Mr. McConkey's frail health would not permit much office work. His strength must be conserved for writing and speaking. Miss McDonald had the same vision for the work as he had, and she realized, perhaps more fully than he, how important it was for him to conserve his physical strength in order to prevent another break-down. She knew that a racking pain in the head inevitably followed too much activity, so she tried to shield him from those who were so enthusiastic about the message that they forgot the man entirely. One such woman came to the office to book him for a certain speaking engagement, and

Miss McDonald replied firmly that he already had as many engagements as his strength would permit, and he could not make them any farther ahead. Whereupon the lady said in great surprise, "Well, doesn't Mr. McConkey go where he is called?" "No," answered the secretary, "he goes where he is sent."

By 1918 the work had gained the momentum of which he had dreamed, as a few of the letters below will attest.

————

"Toronto, Canada.

"You will perhaps remember sending me a few weeks ago Mr. McConkey's little book, *The Threefold Secret of the Holy Spirit*. Never will I be able to thank God enough for being led to send for it; and I thank you so much for the kindly spirit in which it was given. How I have just drunk in every word! Oh, it has enlightened me so! I have prayed so earnestly. I longed for closer communion and to be filled with the Spirit as I have seen in some of God's children; and I have sought it in Pentecostal meetings but I could not go all the way with them, but kept praying in faith that God would satisfy my longing and fulfill the desire of my heart; and now through you and that precious little book, and in His own way, I thank God I know the secret and am abiding in Him by faith, love and prayer, for His continual keeping. I shall always pray God to continue to bless you and the distribution of the little book. Please may I have the companion to it, *The Surrendered Life*, as I see you offer it on same conditions. Thank God, my life is now surrendered. God has given me such a longing to win others for Him. Am giving tracts at every opportunity with prayer. Will you please pray for God's blessing on the effort?"

"New York City

"Sometime in the early spring I got hold of *The Threefold Secret of the Holy Spirit* through the McAuley Mission here in New York. After ten years or more of unsuccessful searching for this truth in Christian Science, New Thought, and other such circles, this book appealed to me tremendously at once.

"In regard to the matter of its circulation, I have gotten it into the hands of a gentleman by the name of William Johnson, who has become greatly interested and who, I believe, has written you. He is becoming a most enthusiastic worker along these lines.

"Would like you to send me the following books to my vacation address given below: *Prayer, The End of the Age, The Surrendered Life.* Am enclosing my check for five dollars for the perpetuation of the good work."

"Minneapolis

"May we have three copies, at least, of *The Threefold Secret of the Holy Spirit?* I want the book put into the hands of every out-going missionary from the Minneapolis Branch. Recently my marked copy was given as a 'voyage package' to one of our women. She writes back in no uncertain words that the book has been a blessing to her. I am longing to have a copy for my own use once more. Each time I read, a new truth, or truth in a new form, comes to me."

"Yonkers, N. Y.

"I have been looking forward to the time when I would be able to thank you in a substantial way for the great helpfulness of your Spirit-filled tracts, which have been handed to me by God's children, and as also sent to me by your Company; but God has not as yet, in His infinite wisdom, seen fit to provide sufficient therefor, but I cannot delay longer thanking one of His saints for his part in helping me through the trials that our heavenly Father has seen fit to permit."

The secret of the joy Mr. McConkey had in all of his work was undoubtedly the recognition of the fact that his only job was to carry messages—no responsibility beyond that, but a very strict obligation to carry each message straight. If he talked with an unsaved man about his soul, or with a Christian about some perplexing problem or crushing burden, or if he addressed groups in person or through the printed page, it was the same thing. He could tell them only what the Lord had told him—what he had actually heard. That meant what he had heeded. Those who read his books sometimes wondered if it were possible for them to be lived out in ordinary flesh-and-blood. But when they knew him, they realized that he was simply too honest to talk above his experience—and that settled it. He always kept a notebook and pencil in his pocket, and whenever any spiritual truth flashed into his soul, he jotted it down at once. "For," he said, "the Lord may not give me that message again."

It was characteristic of him that he never rushed impetuously into any course of action without a clear revelation from the Lord. Whether he was facing a matter of momentous consequence or an issue of lesser moment, he always waited for the Lord to point the way. He believed that God's great clarifier in guidance is—waiting. How beautifully he illustrates this principle is indicated by the following quotation taken from *Guidance*.

"Sometimes you draw from the faucet a glass of water which is muddy and turbid. How do you clear it? You place the glass of muddy water on your table. Moment by moment the sediment deposits at the bottom of the glass. Gradually the water grows clearer. In a few moments it is so clear that you may distinguish objects through it. It has all been brought about simply by waiting. The law is the same in the realm of guidance. Here, too, God's great precipitant is—waiting. We face some situation needing His guidance. It is full of uncertainty. We seek to peer through it as through the glass of turbid water. But we cannot see. The one thing to do is to wait. As we do so the sediment slowly settles. The situation clears. Things take on new proportions, new adjustments. The trifling things assume their proper place of insignificance. Waiting is the solution of it all. The time element is the supremely essential factor. The vast majority of our mistakes come from neglect of it. Haste is more often a trap of Satan than it is a necessity of guidance. 'They which believe shall not make haste,' is true here as in many other crises."

One of his most helpful tracts was written as the direct result of waiting on the Lord for guidance. Sometimes whole months would pass before the Holy Spirit spoke to his soul so clearly that he felt justified in giving his message to the public. One summer, while on vacation, he prayed earnestly that he might receive a message that could be given the printer on his return to Pittsburgh. But there was no word from the Lord except the word to rest and relax mind and body.

Vacation passed, and he started home without tidings. On the way home he stopped over Sunday in a near-by town and heard a local minister speak from the text, "I will give them beauty for ashes." Quick as a flash, he knew that "Beauty for Ashes" was the theme, and soon there followed the outline and the illustrations which go to make up the booklet by that name. I do not know the minister's name or how he treated the subject but, at least, he was the instrument used to suggest the title for a message that has had a life-giving effect on thousands of fainting hearts. So, first of all, the theme must be given definitely by God. The statement, illustration, and application that followed gradually were no less His gift, and all through the writing of each booklet or book was a total dependence on God to use the natural literary gift in such way as to give both force and polish. No message was ever submitted to the printer until it had been worked over carefully. There were enthusiastic friends who would have had each oral message taken down in shorthand and published immediately, but he would not allow this because there are liberties one may take in speaking that are not permissible in writing. And if anything on earth deserved to be clothed in choice language, certainly it was a message from God!

To eloquent, sensational religious leaders, it must have been a tame sight—this quiet, conventional man who did not move out of his position while speaking, used few gestures, and seldom raised his voice, speaking to a little group of church people. But there was never anything tame to *him* about a message. He instinctively sensed that in every group, no matter how small, there were hungry souls—some hungry for salvation, in spite of their church membership, and others hungry for the peace past understanding that can come only through presenting themselves a living sacrifice, holy, acceptable unto God. Furthermore, he knew that the Word would not return void.

And so in his Jerusalem, Judea, and Samaria, the spoken message was heard. There were no spectacular results obtained because there were no high pressure methods used; but power went out through him. Here and there a man or woman went home to the prayer-closet and yielded to God the life hitherto bound by selfishness or worldliness, and because of this the ranks of missionaries and Christian workers at home and abroad were reunited. No occasion for earthly noise, this, but doubtless there was rejoicing in the presence of the angels.

There are preachers who would feel self-condemned for any failure to preach when called upon, but they would not be tremendously concerned about preaching without a special word from God, about running without tidings. But to James McConkey, one was as serious as the other. Once while on a visit to Philadelphia, he called on his dear friend, Dr. D. M. Stearns, who was rector of The Church of the Atonement, in Germantown. It was Saturday afternoon and after they had talked for a while, Mr. McConkey rose to go, when Dr. Stearns asked, "Are you speaking anywhere tomorrow?"

"No, I have no engagements," Mr. McConkey replied.

"Then how would you like to come out and speak to our people? I am going to preach on a text of two words, 'Hitherto . . . Henceforth.' I will speak on

'Hitherto' and you come and speak on 'Henceforth.' "

One of those slow smiles spread over Mr. McConkey's face as he said, "But I have no message on 'Henceforth.' "

Dr. Stearns knew better than to urge, so he simply said, "Well, if you get one, just come on out and speak at the morning service."

He got it, going back on the train that afternoon, and was at the church the next morning to deliver it. For about fifteen minutes, Dr. Stearns preached on "Hitherto hath the Lord helped us" (I Samuel 7:12), giving a striking message on several recurrences of the word *hitherto* in Scripture, after which he said, "Now our Brother McConkey, whom most of you know, will speak on 'Henceforth.' "

Mr. McConkey rose and announced as his text, "Henceforth we should not serve sin" (Rom. 6:6). It was a new text for him but an old theme, and one in which he delighted, for the passion of his life was for purity from sin in the body of Christ. His was a simple but impassioned plea for freedom from the service of Satan. Mrs. Stearns, speaking to him after the service, said, "Well, the Spirit certainly led you two in the most remarkable combination-message these people have ever heard!"

VII

PROGRESS OF THE SILVER PUBLISHING SOCIETY

AN OLD REPORT of the Silver Publishing Society covering the first seven years of its work (1917-1923) gives some interesting facts showing how the Lord's good hand was upon it from the start. We quote a few of them below:

Year	Requests Received	Offerings Received	Books Distributed	Tracts Distributed
1917	13,216	$ 5,651.20	20,000	100,000
1918	19,522	8,541.09	46,000	165,000
1919	27,025	8,834.58	40,707	270,000
1920	33,000	12,316.49	48,000	840,000
1921	44,000	16,543.61	66,000	1,210,000
1922	53,880	19,167.58	75,439	1,285,000
1923	60,128	21,533.96	74,307	1,526,900
	250,771	$92,588.51	370,453	5,396,900

All told, this means that eighty million pages, or about sixty tons of this devotional literature, was sent forth during this period; and practically all of it upon request, thus insuring its reading and safeguarding from waste. The greater part of the receipts each year went for printing and postage. In 1922, for instance, the receipts were something over $19,000 and nearly $14,000 of this was paid to the printer and the postmaster; $2,267.59 went for office salaries, but not a cent to Mr. McConkey. Each year was closed with all bills paid and a small balance. At the close of 1922 there was in the treasury $71.05 with which to begin the new year. But there was also this surety: "God is faithful." During this year, the first editions of *Guidance* and *The Ministry of Suffering* were made. *The Book of Revelation* had appeared in July, 1921. During the following eighteen months, 54,000 copies of it were printed.

Yes, the work was having, not an unhealthy growth, that is invariably ephemeral, but a very steady development. One important element in this growth has not been mentioned—the translations. During these seven years requests for permission to translate and circulate certain of the books and tracts had been steadily coming in, which requests were always granted unless some very unusual circumstance rendered it impracticable. So by 1923, translations had been made into eighteen languages and dialects, some of which were: Chinese, Spanish, German, Swedish, Arabic, Malayalam, Russian, Zulu, French, Portuguese, Hindustani, and Korean. Their circulation was taken care of by individuals or organizations on the foreign field so it was never included in the regular report sent out from the office. In regard to an inquiry from Mr. Herbert Toms, a missionary to Guatemala, concerning a Spanish translation of *The Surrendered Life*, Mr. McConkey wrote: "Dear Brother:

"I would prefer that no translation of my books be

placed in this country in the hands of any publishing firm who would sell them, as our books are all given away free that 'the gospel might be without price.' Mr. R. D. Smith, Bible House of Los Angeles, California, however, publishes and distributes free in Spanish, my books on the Holy Spirit and Prayer and would have my consent to publish your translation of *The Surrendered Life*, if it is acceptable to him."

Later, came a request for permission to translate *all* of Mr. McConkey's works into Arabic, to be used in Syria. At first, it seemed wise to stipulate that the translations be circulated free, on just the same plan as those sent out from the home base, but numerous cases began to arise where it seemed practical to charge a nominal sum for the books and tracts in other languages, rather than to give them free. This foreign policy was set forth in a letter to Pastor Th. Arvidson, Stockholm, Sweden, which ran:

"Oct. 6, 1920

"Dear Brother:

"We have adopted a permanent policy for our foreign translations and would kindly request you to ignore our former letter in this matter and note the following:

"We gladly give you permission to translate my book on the Holy Spirit under the following conditions: (1) We would much prefer that the book be circulated free if at all possible. (2) If this is not possible, then circulate it in the best manner you can as the Lord leads you. (3) In case you use the sale edition, rather than a free one, we reserve the right to grant permission for a free edition if the Lord should open the way through someone else.

"We feel this plan is absolutely fair to both of us and trust it will be satisfactory to you.

"Cordially yours,
"James H. McConkey"

How the author's heart leaped when these requests came! And how he might have let some personal ambition creep in as the tide of popularity increased if he had not kept each book and tract where it had been placed at its birth—*on the altar!* They were no longer his. If the Lord chose to use His own property in a wide way, then praise the Lord! How he watched for the reception each message would meet as it went forth!

The Threefold Secret was usually the leader, with *The Surrendered Life* following close. *The End of the Age* and *The Book of Revelation* were translated into Swedish by Mr. August Stromstedt, of Kristenham, Sweden, in 1922. The study of prophecy was gaining ground in the United States, and how heartening it was to know that it was also becoming more acceptable abroad! His heart glowed with each testimony to the way the messages were being used in foreign lands, for paradoxically, they *were his,* just as flesh-and-blood children of consecrated Christians are still theirs, although the children have been given back to God, laid on the altar—theirs to send out into the world to be used of Him for His glory.

It was distressing when requests for money to help in translations had to be refused. One such came in 1923 from Mr. D. L. Pierson of the American Christian Literature Society for Moslems, asking permission to translate *The Threefold Secret* into Persian, to be used among Christian converts. He wrote:

"Many of these come from Mohammedanism and need very much to have their spiritual life strengthened, and to understand the teachings of the Bible in regard to the Holy Spirit, and I am writing to know if there is any way in which you could help these missionaries in Persia to give the book to Christians over there. The cost is estimated at about $1400.00."

Mr. McConkey wrote back on April 21, 1923:

"I wish indeed we were able to assist in the Persian translation for we would gladly do so if possible. We have, however, received twenty-five thousand letters of request for our literature in the last four months and the demand is so tremendous that our funds are at the lowest possible ebb and it is beyond our power to do anything more at this time in furthering the circulation of the Persian translation.

"If anything develops in the near future along this line, we shall be more than glad to advise you of it."

It is interesting to note that on the Board of the Society (or "Company") making this request was Mrs. William Borden, the mother of William, the "Borden of Yale." Many reading *Borden of Yale* were interested in *The Threefold Secret* because this young man's life had been profoundly influenced by its message, and wrote to ask for a copy of it.

Uninformed friends often got the impression that "faith work" was very easy work because all that was required was to present petitions and they would be granted in short order. The only obligation resting on the Silver Publishing Company was to ask God for money and the desired amounts would flow in and the books flow out. This, of course in the final analysis, was true, but they failed to take account of the fact that this kind of prayer must be put under God's searchlight, that the lives of those doing the praying must meet the Scriptural requirements of John 15:7: "If ye abide in me, and my words abide in you, ye shall ask what ye will and it shall be done unto you." Even when this was done, there might be long periods of testing—by waiting and by denial of specific requests. It was thus in the matter mentioned above. No doubt Mr. McConkey would have preferred that every order be filled immediately, that financial help be furnished Christian organizations that wished to put out certain translations; but God did not always will it so. There were times when financial pressure forced more and more prayer and brought more and more faith in a God who sometimes denied a petition even though He answered the man. At times there was nothing to do but accept "No" as the answer for the present. But the office force could always pray with assurance that *one* definite petition would be granted; that sufficient offerings would be received to maintain the work, that requests for literature would continue and that the supply would meet the demand. If the Lord had refused to honor this prayer, the doors would have closed. Certainly no debt would have been rashly incurred in order to carry on. If the Lord had withheld necessary funds, the plain implication would have been that He wanted the work stopped, never that He wanted a loan secured. So activity continued, sometimes on the narrowest of margins, but always without debt.

By the latter part of 1922 the work seemed sufficiently established to warrant incorporation. Therefore, on December 30 of that year the Common Pleas Court of Allegheny County approved the application and the Silver Publishing Society became incorporated. The purpose of the organization, as given in the charter, is for "the publication and distribution, without profit, of religious literature." It was deemed wise to change "Company" to "Society," as the former term might be interpreted to mean a business firm conducted for profit. The names of the subscribers were: James H. McConkey, Walter P. Fraser, Clark M. Kefover, W. McConkey Kerr, and Winifred E. McDonald. When the Board of Directors was formed, Mr. McConkey was elected president, Mr. Fraser, vice-president, and Miss McDonald, secretary-treasurer.

Mr. McConkey assigned to the Silver Publishing Society all copyrights issued to him on all his books and booklets, and all his interests in writings not copyrighted. As far as the world was concerned, he conducted the affairs of the office on business principles. That is, he never asked favors of, or expected reductions from business firms because it was a religious institution. Every bill was paid promptly, as no obligation was contracted until sufficient funds were on hand to meet it. Strict account was kept of all money received and expended. On the other hand, if some of the worldly-wise had known that it was a "business" without capital-visible, tangible capital—that each year the work began with a balance of one hundred dollars or less, they might have had something to say. But the Silver Publishing Society met the business world on its own terms and looked to God for means to carry the work daily, not for liquidation of debts accumulated.

In January of 1926, Miss McDonald found it necessary to resign, and her place was taken by Mr. Howard A. Banks (afterwards, Howard A. Banks, Litt.D.), long-time friend of Mr. McConkey, who remained in the office until December, 1928, and from that time until his death in June, 1932, kept a watchful eye upon everything connected with the work. A whole book might be written on the friendship of these two men, which began some thirty years before when Mr. Banks was a newspaper man in Charlotte, North Carolina. Mr. Banks was the son of a Presbyterian minister, and a Christian before Mr. McConkey crossed his path; but as he once said in a testimony meeting at Keswick, New Jersey, he entered the victorious life by way of prophecy, and Mr. McConkey was used to open his eyes to the glorious truths in connection with the Lord's return. Later, Mr. Banks himself, became an excellent Bible teacher, but he always insisted on maintaining the attitude of a pupil where Mr. McConkey was concerned. His devotion and admiration grew as their association became closer; nothing ever dimmed the ardor of Howard Banks for his best friend, and perhaps there was nothing in the life of James McConkey more beautiful than this friendship. Mr. McConkey soon discovered Mr. Banks's gift for devotional and expository writing. He had a way of discovering talents without seeming to advise at all, or helping to direct those talents in the God-planned way. He encouraged Mr. Banks to find an outlet in Christian periodicals. This led to an associate-editorship of the *Sunday School Times,* and finally to the editing of *Christ Life* maga-

zine. So, when he came to the office of the Silver
Publishing Society, it was with the understanding that
it was part-time work, that half of the day would be
reserved for editorial duties.

How grateful to God Mr. McConkey was on that
January day when he announced to Richmond friends
that the responsibility of the office work would now
be upon "younger and stronger shoulders" than his,
for he not only trusted Mr. Banks's personal devotion
to him but was confident of his judgment as well. He
knew that, in most cases, their reactions would be
identical, and if there were complicated matters re-
quiring prayer and waiting on God, these would be
presented to him before action was taken. So it was
a tremendous relief to be rid of these responsibilities,
and to give himself more completely to the writing of
new messages. He was spending time now in Norfolk,
Petersburg and Richmond, delivering addresses, writing messages and holding conferences with those who
came to him for advice. Constantly the way was opening for a wider ministry, although the physical strength
was so limited.

There was still the old thorn in the flesh, his inability to write more than twenty or thirty minutes a
day without bringing on a fearful headache that completely unfitted him for any work whatsoever. But he
had learned to use the Ediphone and had found that
speaking did not tire him nearly as much as writing,
and in this way he was accomplishing more in the
same length of time than if he undertook to write out
each message. Those who have never known from experience the real meaning of a nervous headache could
hardly understand why Mr. McConkey was accounted

a semi-invalid when he was seldom confined to bed. He did not complain, so friends were naturally perplexed when he sorrowfully refused so many speaking engagements. But intimate friends recognized the expression of suffering on the face which meant that the head had been overtaxed and the pain had set in. There was nothing to do for it, the doctors could recommend nothing but rest. Even among those who loved him most there were few who understood in any measure what the physical suffering meant and how disheartening was the curtailment of activities in which he longed so much to be engaged.

So, while Mr. McConkey was using his small measure of strength chiefly for writing and speaking, Mr. Banks was promoting the circulation of the messages. This, like other phases of the work, was chiefly a matter of asking, and then waiting to see the goodness of God. No effort was made to secure translations of books and pamphlets, but it was amazing how requests for permissions which had been coming steadily for years, now began to multiply.

In July, 1927, Mr. Watkins R. Roberts, Director of the North East India General Mission, wrote:
"My dear Brother Banks:
"There are at least eleven important languages in India in which there is very little devotional literature available; indeed it appears now that the Christian Publishing Organizations are determined to thrust upon the Indian Christians the Modernistic trash that comes from the West. We would like therefore to issue editions of from 3,000 to 6,000 copies of as many of the publications (McConkey) as possible in these languages. We would also require fairly large editions

in English and could very easily circulate at least 6,000 of each book and tract. It would of course be impossible for such an extensive work to be handled from America and our desire therefore was that the Evangelical Literature Trust be allowed to do this from Calcutta. The only difficulty, of course, is the finance.

"Believe me, the need is really greater today than it has ever been before. We are up against a deliberate attempt to undermine the Christian faith and to introduce Modernism in all its false forms into this country. I would very earnestly hope and pray that the Lord may make it possible for you to coöperate with us and perhaps find some among His stewards who will desire to become the Lord's channel for this purpose."

The first steward to respond was James H. Mc-Conkey—with a draft, first for twenty-five dollars and another for one hundred. In his letter of thanks, Mr. Roberts said:

"*The Threefold Secret* is already in the press. My purpose is to issue at once as many as we can get for $100.00. The message is too precious to be delayed. This is surely a token that the Lord means for India, Burma and Ceylon to have Mr. McConkey's booklets on a more extensive scale than ever before."

Some time before this, a letter had come from Dr. D. H. Dolman, in Wandsbek, Germany, introducing himself as one of "Keswick's own" missionaries, working among the Jews in Germany and asking permission to translate the books and tracts into German for use in his Christian magazine. The permission was given and in the summer of 1928, Dr. Dolman's desire to meet face to face the man whose books had so influenced his own life and had been so used in the lives of his parishioners, was also granted.

He and Mr. McConkey met that summer in the home of Mr. and Mrs. Mortimer B. Lane, at Eaglesmere, Pa., and became fast friends. They were different types, naturally, these two. Mr. McConkey, tall and reserved, Dr. Dolman, rotund, ruddy and smiling. But after you had talked with both for five minutes, you knew they were of one mind and one spirit. At one of the conferences where Dr. Dolman spoke that summer (not Eaglesmere), there were certain features on the program that could hardly be termed spiritual. For instance, one night a season of joke-telling had been planned in the living-room of the hotel just after the evening service, which was to close at nine o'clock. But Dr. Dolman spoke that night on the Holy Spirit, and the message must have gone home. Without a word being said, there appeared to be a general conviction of inconsistency in the program; and those who had planned the merriment went quietly to their rooms for meditation. It was at this conference that I met Dr. Dolman, and I remember now how his face lighted up when I spoke of his new-found friend, and he said, "Oh, *dear* Brother James!"

While Dr. Dolman was multiplying the ministry of the messages by means of German translations, the Reverend Peter Gorodishz, F.R.G.S., in the neighboring country of Poland, had realized their value to his fellow-countrymen and sent the following letter to the office:

"Dear Brethren in Christ:

"Surely you know that the Jew is a great friend of books; he loves reading, and when he receives from the

Mission a book or tract which tells him of the Messiah in popular language, this does not remain without good results. To our great regret, we ought to state that the distribution of good Christian literature to the Jews, in Yiddish, is much neglected. Because of our mission journeys through the country we are those who distribute most of Christian literature to the Jews. We opened a printing work in Bialystok to meet this need. We publish Christian tracts with good contents, and in pure Yiddish, for circulation among the Jews. Experience has taught us that a small tract or a book written by a Gentile Christian which explains salvation in Christ, brings great blessing to the Jews.

"Now, dear brethren, comes the chief reason why I am writing to you. I have read many of your valuable tracts. I have found a number of them would be very suitable for translation into Yiddish and circulation among the Jews. Your tracts are especially suitable for the Jews because of their good examples, and the Jews love such as the following tracts: *If We Neglect, Law and Grace, Holy Ground, Give God a Chance, The Fifth Sparrow, The Father's House, In and Out, Believing Is Seeing.* We want very much for you to give us a chance to publish all of these tracts in Yiddish. We shall translate them and print them in our printing works.

"Our appeal to you has come after much consideration. It is very pressing because the winter is at an end; with the beginning of spring will commence our missionary tours with the Gospel cars, and we need Christian tracts. Please do not consider our appeal as something very common. We have much considered it, and only after signs from the Lord that we may do it, we appeal to you. Help us to give the Jews a chance to recognize their Messiah, to find peace for their souls in the salvation completed on Golgotha."

Needless to say, this permission was joyfully granted.

Time would fail to tell of all the requests for permission to translate; so we shall mention only a few others. One was from Jonathan M. Eujita, who modestly said, "I am a Japanese Christian minister who speaks some English; and I should like, with your permission, to translate some, or all, of your tracts." A few months later came a similar one from Miss Sadie Lea Weidner, an American missionary to Japan, putting special emphasis on *The Way of Victory*, which she had just read for the first time. Miss Weidner went on to say that a great number of the workers used of God in Japan believed and taught the doctrine of eradication of the sinful nature, and for this reason there was a special need for this very message.

Dr. A. V. Dobrini, from Poland, wrote:

"We would inquire if you would be so very kind as to allow us to translate some of your works into Russian and to publish them as far as God gives us the time and means for doing so. This would be of very great blessing for numberless Russian believers, and the good seeds would bear fruit for a long time.

"While I know how very much occupied your time is, I also know your kindness, and my prayer is that the Lord may put into your heart His decision as to what is to be done."

A native missionary in Brazil next entreated for the circulation of *The Threefold Secret* "in a Catholic land where they have *no* idea whatever of the Holy Spirit," and then suggested that the work of translation be turned over to a brother pastor of his "who is recognized as an excellent pen in Portuguese, and a devout Christian, and his orthodoxy is as sound as Moody's."

And so they kept coming, these requests, each one bringing a real joy to the soul of the author. He seldom mentioned them unless the person to whom he was talking had shown a vital interest in the work as a whole. Boasting was excluded from this as well as from everything else. It was all the marvelous grace of God that such simple Gospel messages could be used all over the world! But the deep, throbbing joy that came whenever a message was sent into a new field of service, only those know, who have seen the Lord use that which has been given back to Him!

And one of the greatest joys of all was to think that the printed messages could go to the remote places of earth where his frail body could never have gone. One "Sister Mary," evidently of the Lutheran Church, wrote from Australia to tell how she had used the tracts as follow-ups in her personal work, how the natives, in some of her outposts, were trying to keep the meetings going and were using the booklets for their sermons. A young African in a Christian library in Nigeria, after expressing his gratitude for the books and tracts in English, wrote:

"If you do not have your tracts and books translated into our own tongue, may I help you in doing so? If so, kindly send those you like to be thus translated with papers to me, and I will do it for you free of all charges, *gratis*.

"The two young Christian brothers, whose letters are enclosed here with mine, are greatly interested in these books and tracts, and they desired greatly to have the same. They are traveling evangelists. Thanking you for humanity—"

A native Japanese missionary who had been granted permission to translate the book *Prayer* wrote back to express his appreciation and to ask if he might be permitted to sell it. In his letter, he said, "I have no money for printing, and besides I have nobody to support me but God. I am praying just now for the need for printing." He was given permission to make a "small charge" which would help cover the cost.

Many other letters were received asking permission to translate Mr. McConkey's messages into foreign languages, and the office records show that eighteen of these were completed; whether others who were granted permission ever acted upon it is not known.

He was keenly aware of the danger of leaving his testimony entirely with the printed page and realized that he himself must deal daily with those who were out of Christ and give them the Gospel personally. Naturally, he considered that those who crossed his path in the daily routine were his first responsibility. One of these was a drayman who called several times each week to deliver the mail bags of literature to the Post Office Station. Mr. McConkey, for several afternoons stayed at the office late so he might have time to make a friendly contact with this man and after the first few times, he began to speak of spiritual things. The giving of the Gospel to him was followed as usual by earnest prayer and a reminder to the Father of the promise that His word should not return void. One day after an office prayer-meeting, he rose from his knees saying, "I must speak to him again today.

I believe he is near a decision. As we prayed, assurance seemed so definite."

When the drayman came and greetings had been exchanged, Mr. McConkey laid his hand upon the man's shoulder and said, "Brother, I would be happy to know your decision today."

"I have been thinking about what you said to me," he replied, "and I want to know Him as my Savior too—this moment. I am sure of His love for me."

Much of the united prayer that went up from the office necessarily was for money. He often spoke to Miss McDonald of the influence which the story of George Muller's life had had on his own prayer life; and of his assurance that all needs of the Silver Publishing Society would be provided since that day on the mountain-top when he had dedicated to the Lord the first small amount received as an offering to his work. In this connection he said to her, "You know God delights in surprising His children. This same Father who arrayed the lilies in spotless white—adding fragrance—clothed the birds in beautiful plumage—giving them the gift of song for our enjoyment—promises to supply every need. In giving, He is never impoverished." One of his favorite poems and one of which he often reminded himself before going to prayer was from John Newton which runs:

"*Thou art coming to a King,*
Large petitions with thee bring,
For His grace and power are such
None can ever ask too much."

There were many unavoidable interruptions in the office work, but he did not seem to mind any of them and here, as in every other place, he welcomed the presence of children. Jennie and Eldon Wright, the children of a minister who at that time was doing Jewish Mission work in Pittsburgh, came regularly on Saturdays to help with mailing out the books and tracts. These children sometimes drew others among whom was the little five-year-old daughter of an insurance agent in the Bessemer Building. One day she came just a few minutes before time for the group to kneel in prayer so she was invited to kneel with them. (In the group were Mr. McConkey, Miss McDonald, the secretary, Miss Marie Devedeaux, the mailing clerk, who was a happy convert from French Catholicism, Alta Sipe, the typist, and Jennie and Eldon.) After that, she proved to be a throbbing question mark as to how God "away up in the sky" could hear and answer prayer and send money to send books everywhere. Mr. McConkey told her the story of Peter and his dilemma about the tribute money, as recorded in the seventeenth chapter of Matthew, placing emphasis upon the fact that Christ knew the existent need before Peter spoke of it ("Jesus prevented him"), and He knew Peter's thoughts. She wanted to know, of course, whether God knew her thoughts and then in beautiful fashion, he unfolded to her the Gospel story.

Sometimes the visitors to the office were Christians of the most mature kind, missionaries and other Christian leaders who themselves were prayer-warriors. Among these were Dr. Charles Abel of Papua, Dr. Stephens of the Great Commission Prayer League, Dr. Charles Blanchard of Wheaton College, Dr. Henry W. Frost of the China Inland Mission, and Dr. E. J. Pace, the well-known cartoonist of the Sunday School Times.

These contacts were refreshing to him especially as much of his time was given to spiritual babes.

Many of these "babes" were known to him only through correspondence; they had never felt the touch of his hand or heard the sound of his voice but they had come to know the inner man by means of his books and they wrote freely as if to an intimate friend. Some of the most interesting letters came from native Christians in Africa who had employed the village scribe to do the writing. As a rule, these scribes had a most limited knowledge of English and expressed their thoughts very quaintly. The transformation from darkness to light by means of the gospel message was very marked and gratitude was expressed in various ways. Some wrote that they had become humble slaves to their newly-found Savior and also to the Christian friends who had been the means of leading them to Him, so they wished to make gifts to the office. One offered to send monkey skins for a coat because he had received garments of salvation; however, the skins did not pass customs so were destroyed or returned. Another sent an English hard-tack can of African tiger nuts (much like cocoanuts), which Mr. McConkey peeled with his knife for the benefit of the office force. Occasionally the African friends applied the promise, "Ask and ye shall receive," by asking gifts from the office, such things as fountain pens and footballs. These requests, of course, must be refused but whether they fully understood or not, their ardor did not seem to cool. Their "blessing letters" were among the most cherished.

Trials of various kinds were not lacking but he accepted each one as from God, as a part of his training, realizing that by experiencing the comfort of the Holy Spirit, one was enabled unto a more effectual ministry to others as a result of the grace and strength given. He often quoted, ". . . . who comforteth us in all our tribulations that we may be able to comfort them which are in any trouble by the comfort wherewith we ourselves are comforted of God." The death of Gustave Moline, who had been the office secretary until he entered Wheaton College preparatory to medical missionary service in China, was one such trial. Gustave, who was one of his favorite boys and had every sign of spiritual promise, was taken ill with pneumonia during his first year in college, and did not recover. His former chief was deeply affected— said he could not understand why one with such a definite call and whose life held so much promise should be taken Home, but he added, "God always knows best. His understanding is infinite and we, His children, should never say 'Why?' to Him. Our sorrow and loss is his gain. To be with Christ is far better."

Harder even than the sorrow of parting from dear friends, sometimes, was the criticism which came from other Christians, from those very people who might have been expected to support him. One of these wrote him a very harsh letter, criticizing one of his prophetic books. After it had been read and laid on the desk, he remarked that the Christian often learned lessons of obedience, humility and love from criticism—by the Father's permissive will; the fruit of discipleship is love of the brethren and this love is one of the fruits of the Holy Spirit shed abroad in our hearts. God chooses to enrich our lives through experiences of every type—as we are yielding to Him and He has added the promise, "Afterwards, it yieldeth the peaceable fruits of righteousness."

VIII

VARIED MISSIONS OF THE GOD-GIVEN MESSAGES

A CASUAL observer sitting in the little two-room office of the Bessemer Building and noting the volume of mail that was deposited there every day might not be impressed with the significance of it. If he regarded these books and tracts as just more printed matter or even as "more religious books," there could be no thrill in watching the increase of mail at the office of the Silver Publishing Society. Not so the author and staff and outside friends who knew them as messages from God by means of which their whole lives had been changed. To them, there was a thread of romance through it all. Each letter of request represented an infinitely valuable soul, each book or tract sent in response could, and should be, the means of satisfying the need of that soul, of imparting new purpose to life and the will to carry it out.

It was interesting to watch for "blessing letters" from those who had not requested books themselves, but who had been handed one by someone else, or had come into possession of one, seemingly by chance. Miss Ethel Laros, who at one time was employed in the office, tells of a letter from a janitor's wife, in which she says

her husband found one of the McConkey books in the
waste-basket and brought it home. It helped her so
much that she wanted others. One young woman who
was led to surrender her life, to find her life-work,
and to realize how Christ makes all things new, told
the author that she had never been able to find out who
sent her the first of the books, but having read one, she
kept on until she had read all.

These are typical cases and confirmed Mr. Mc-
Conkey's conviction that it was the will of God for
his books to be circulated on a large scale rather than
to use the restricted method of Mr. Kelker. This difference of opinion, however, was not a "sharp conten-
tion" like that between Paul and Barnabas. Until his
death in 1928, Mr. Kelker kept sending out the
McConkey books and tracts in small quantities along
with those by other authors, while the Silver Publishing
Society was the exclusive agency for circulating Mr.
McConkey's messages in large quantities. Meanwhile,
the same loving intimacy was maintained between the
two friends, Mr. McConkey being a frequent visitor
in the Kelker home, where he was known to the children as "Uncle Jim." The following bits are chosen
from their correspondence a few months before Mr.
Kelker's death:

"June 1, 1928

"Dear Brother Fred:

"The North East India General Mission are asking
permission to translate my messages into the vernacular
and to reprint some in English for use among their
local converts. I am strongly inclined to grant their
request, specializing that they limit the circulation of
the English messages to their own work in India, in

order that we may be completely safeguarded here and in England in our work. Would this be all right, to your mind? Let me have your reaction.

"We send the enclosed order and check for $5.00 to yourself for handling. Just let me have a word, Freddie dear, as to how you are. I think often of you and always with the same old love. Howard (Mr. Banks) joins me in affectionate good wishes to all of you.

"Lovingly,

"Brother Jim"

"Dear Old Jimmie:

"It is perfectly all right to permit 'General Mission' to reprint your messages, but make it plain it is *restricted* to their work in India. Am better, but still *restricted* in work and active service except the tract work. Hallelujah! All send love to you and Brother Banks.

"As ever in Him,

"Fred"

So, while Mr. Kelker was sending out individual copies of the books and tracts from Harrisburg, the Silver Publishing Society was filling orders for hundreds and sometimes thousands. If a pastor would ask for a hundred for his church members, Mr. Kelker would write the pastor to tell his people about the tract and if they wanted it, to write for it. He felt that much Christian literature was wasted by being sent in large quantities, and that this method might prevent such waste. Mr. McConkey thought the wider distribution would compensate for whatever loss might be involved.

A few facts gleaned from letters to the Silver Publishing Society will seem to bear out Mr. McConkey's conviction. From the leader of a woman's prayer group in Collingswood, New Jersey:

"We have been using a copy of Mr. McConkey's book, *Prayer*, as a guide to our study. This book has proved such a blessing to all that many have expressed a desire to have a copy of their own. As mine was secured a great many years ago, I am writing to find out if it is still available and if so, how I may obtain a dozen copies."

Among others who wanted to use *Prayer* in large quantities, was a Covenant of Prayer Secretary for a Presbyterial organization in Los Angeles, who wrote:

"We trust that every one of our 118 missionary societies may become a missionary intercessor. Many Covenant of Prayer leaders have asked for literature. Your book, *Prayer*, seems the answer to that query. I have secured eight copies from the Bible House, but I believe there will be many more who will want the book. If so, may I send to you for as many as are needed?"

Wherever leaders in Y.M.C.A.'s had felt the power of Mr. McConkey's oral messages, the books and tracts were sure to be in demand—so across the continent, the calls came. A religious work secretary from Flint, Mich., wrote:

"We are still on the firing-line with the little book, *Prayer*. We would like you to send another hundred copies. The Lord is wonderfully blessing our work. The little book gives us wonderful contact with the men. We have been able to lead numbers into the Christian life and into fellowship with the church."

Occasionally those who wished to use the tracts in very large quantities wrote ahead to ask the actual cost of such a number so they might send an offering commensurate with the request. In cases such as these, the only common sense thing to do was to comply with the request. But usually each person sent what he could, if he sent anything, and asked for what he wanted—and received it if it was available. From the pastor of the First Baptist Church in Hollywood came the following:

"I am planning to visit the entire membership of my church this fall, and I should be very happy to leave in every home a copy of *The Blessing of Doing*. To that end, will you, if it is at all possible, mail me five hundred copies, and I shall be glad to pay for them if you will tell me the price."

Another minister from Waco, Texas, wrote:

"I am this month sending out a series of tracts to ministers in Texas and out of the State. I am exceedingly anxious to get your tract, *The Spirit Filled Life*, in order that I might put one in each envelope sent.

"I am asking you for 2,000 of these tracts if you can possibly spare them for this purpose. I realize the great need now is for revival among ministers. With your coöperation, I am in a position to get your truth circulated intensely through this section. God bless you for the great work you are doing."

Here is another from a pastor of a Presbyterian church in Louisville, Kentucky, asking for 160 copies of *The Book of Revelation* to use in his mid-week prayer-meetings through the fall and winter, and offering to defray the cost. A letter was sent him giving the cost as seven or eight cents a copy, depending on the paper used. This was purely the price of printing without any allowance for overhead.

A Swedish friend in Rockford, Illinois, wrote a friend in Pittsburgh, and the following letter was passed on to the office:

"Do you think it is possible for me to get three hundred copies of McConkey's book about the Holy Spirit? I should like to place a copy of it with every family of my church and also a copy in the hands of each of the young people. If that is possible, will you be kind and arrange so that they will be sent to me? Furthermore, do you think the Silver Publishing Society would allow me to translate the book into Swedish for the little church paper I get out once a month and distribute free in my church?"

From Bible conferences all over the country came requests for tracts in large quantities. When enthusiastic McConkey readers met, they would often discuss their favorites among the books and tell how such-and-such a book or tract had come at just the crucial moment in their lives.

One woman, after pouring into Mr. McConkey's ears her gratitude for *all* of them, said, "But after all, Mr. McConkey, I think *The God Planned Life* is the best of the smaller books."

"I believe it is," he answered.

This little book, like the rest, had been conceived at a mighty cost and was given to the public first in the form of an address. Before it was printed he gave the message in a college chapel in a little town in Alabama one Sunday afternoon. No one seemed particularly impressed or took the trouble to say that the message had gone "home." Heavy-hearted, the speaker walked home by the side of his hostess, the wife of one of the professors. In the lightest of tones she said, "That was a nice little talk you gave us, Mr. McConkey."

"Nice little talk!" A message on which time and tears had been spent lavishly, teaching which could not possibly have been given if he had not first recognized and accepted the plan for his own life, a thing which, at first, had cut so deep that the scar would never be obscured. So that was all it meant to her! Perhaps it was all it would mean to anybody but himself. Perhaps, after all, the Lord would not use it. Later, however, it was printed in tract form, and "blessing letters" regarding it began to come. Moreover, two years after it was given in the little Alabama town, Mr. McConkey received a letter from a woman in another State, reading: "You don't know who I am, but I listened to you give an address on the 'God-planned Life' in ———, Alabama, some time ago and I have never been the same since. It caused me to turn over my life to the Lord completely, and now I am happy in His blessed service. Another woman who was with me that day also received untold blessing, and since then has been able to lead her son to the Lord."

Never thereafter did he have any anxiety about whether the Lord would use a message faithfully recorded and faithfully given. He once said he had learned a lesson from the enemy in the parable of the sower—that the enemy sowed tares *and went his way*. He did not worry because he knew they would come up. On the other hand, many of God's servants sowed the Word, and then agonized about results when they should have been equally as sure their seed would grow.

There was an indefinable quality in his intimate, personal style which made it easy for weary hearts, or hearts relieved of their burden, to approach him and desire a closer acquaintance. The widow of a Methodist minister from Indiana wrote that of all the books she had read, none gave her so much pure gospel as McConkey's, and then she went on to say: "I think *The Threefold Secret* is the best book I have ever read. It is next to my Bible with me and I really think McConkey is a second Paul. I would like to know more about his history. Have you his life story in print? If so, I should like to have it."

Limited strength forbade his answering letters, but they were always answered from the office, and every request for prayer noted and placed before the Lord. When requests for the story of his life came, there was nothing to be sent but the printed slip containing a few general facts about his life and ministry. He had allowed this to be printed doubtless as a means of answering those who must have something about the author, but it was never his idea to have any attention attracted to himself. He was only a voice in the wilderness—all he desired was to be heard. Those who knew him intimately can easily imagine how he would have recoiled at the mere suggestion of a biography in his lifetime, and an autobiography was unthinkable!

He was not at all concerned about readers becoming acquainted with the author, but only about their knowing *Him*, who was the theme of each book and tract, so letters such as this from the head of the Department of Science in a Minneapolis high school delighted his soul most:

"I had been deeply impressed by the subject of sanctification, yet rejected it as impracticable and unattainable, mainly through erroneous teaching and preaching. A second time aroused to a new consideration of it, I was faced once more with what seemed insurmountable difficulties before I saw the clear light by means of *The Threefold Secret of the Holy Spirit.* One day after having pondered the whole matter, I fully yielded to the Lord and there in the quiet of the night, I experienced the fullness of the Spirit. Naturally, I am anxious to see others come into the same blessed experience, and so am enclosing a little money to help along your good work. I am starting in a small way an agency for the distribution of Christian literature, and I imagine you have no objection to my putting in a supply of Mr. McConkey's leaflets and books. Of course you will want to be assured that such literature will be distributed free and not sold. I am superintendent of a Sunday school and my new experience has made me solicitous to lead my staff of officers and teachers into a like experience."

That was the way it worked. One man having yielded his life, straightway would go after others, like Andrew of old. Mr. McConkey had no thought of founding a denomination, or even of beginning a movement. The prime purpose of his life was to lead those who were already in churches to the place where they would become truly useful members of the Church, the body of Christ, meanwhile making plain the requirements for membership in that body so that the untaught might not be left without adequate light on the subject.

Mr. McConkey believed that often God used several instruments in the conversion of a soul; he was slow to think that either his personal influence or his books had been the sole means of winning one to Christ. A young woman once told him during a private conference that his books and the influence of her precious mother had caused her to become a Christian. He turned to her with an understanding smile and said, "I am happy to know that my books were a little supplement to your precious mother's teaching." The girl knew that this was no blandishment; he meant it when he said he was always used along with some other instrument; and appreciating filial love as he did, he felt honored to have his influence placed alongside her mother's. When he received letters telling of blessing received, he never for a moment thought his book was the *only* means of grace, even though the writer mentioned no other. Usually the letters were from Christians who had been led into fullness of life by surrender, but occasionally there was one such as the following, which told of conversion:

"Thank God there are men in this world who have given their lives to the work you are doing. Thank God for those who live Christ-like lives and so bring out of misery and suffering and monstrous sin the very ones that He died on Calvary's cross to save. Two weeks ago today, in the face of supreme difficulties, I gave my whole life to Jesus Christ.

"I received the booklets you so kindly sent me and want to thank you a thousand times for them. On Tuesday night after the books came on Monday, I was to lead a cottage prayer meeting in my neighborhood. Then the booklet, *Prayer*, came as manna from heaven to me."

A pastor from Ohio wrote:

"All your tracts are golden gems but may I tell you of the work accomplished by *Give God A Chance*? One day while listening to a number of men tell the vile stories of their lives, I noticed one man used the expression of 'taking a chance at anything.' Later I sent him a copy of *Give God A Chance* with an invitation to come to our services, and he was converted. He told me it was the result of the little pamphlet."

If Mr. McConkey had been telling this incident, no doubt he would have emphasized the pastor's faithful preaching of the Word, and would have shown how God used this, together with the printed message, to accomplish the salvation of this soul.

Pastors who were too honest to claim experiences they had not really known, but who coveted the highest for themselves and their people, were perhaps the most grateful class. They knew that the spiritual leaders— in their churches — those who did not work in the energy of the flesh but allowed the Spirit to work through them—loved Mr. McConkey's messages. Many of these ministers were brought for the first time into an intelligent appreciation of prophecy through these books. From Arizona came this testimony:

"Permit me to say that *The Book of Revelation*, by Mr. McConkey, is the finest thing I ever read on the subject, and the only book I ever read that gave me any light on that most wonderful of the Books of the Bible. I have been using the outlines as given in this pamphlet in my weekly Bible studies, and the people have been simply captivated."

IX

THE BRAILLE CIRCULATING LIBRARY

When suddenly an ideal takes the form of a reality, a peculiar reaction takes place. So when there appeared in one of the Richmond newspapers, set off in a neat little rectangle, the notice that James H. McConkey would speak on Sunday afternoon in the auditorium of the Central Y.M.C.A., there was a conflict of emotions as I read it. Naturally I was delighted with the opportunity to hear the writer who, in my judgment, stood above all other spiritual authors. But mingled with this was a vague fear that he might not measure up to his books!

When Sunday afternoon came, the auditorium was about full. Three or four men were on the platform, and I scanned them with an examining eye to decide which was he. Not one of them *looked* quite the part! Finally the preliminaries were over, and Mr. McConkey rose to speak—the tall, gray-haired, gray-mustached, serious-faced one of the group. He announced his subject as "The End of the Age, or The Second Coming of Christ," and my feathers fell! Why had he chosen a subject so uninteresting? Of course everyone knows the world is coming to an end sometime, but nobody knows when and the Bible is so difficult to understand that really you couldn't get enough out of it to make any difference! Why had he not elected to speak on some sublime topic like prayer or surrender, on which he could write so beautifully? But, as he went on, reasoning each step of the way, proving each statement by the Scriptures, it became apparent that there *were some things* about the End-time that are knowable, that it must be a subject of importance and one worthy of study or it would not have been mentioned in the Bible more than three hundred times. As I recall it now, it must have been a masterly address but at the time it was disappointing, for I had never before heard a sermon on the subject and was hardly an interested listener. Therefore, partly through disappointment and partly through timidity, I went away without telling him what his books had meant to me, something I had longed to do for several years.

The next fall, after some little contact with the blind of Richmond, I familiarized myself with statistics setting forth the need for Christian literature in Braille. It occurred to me that the best service I could possibly render the blind would be to have the McConkey books put into Braille for them. Accordingly, I wrote to Mr. McConkey suggesting he have some of his pamphlets transcribed into Braille and sent out from his office in Pittsburgh. He replied promptly, saying that he expected to be in Richmond for some weeks during the winter and that when he came, we might talk over the matter.

February arrived and so did Mr. McConkey! An appointment was made for three o'clock Sunday afternoon, February 8 (1925), in the Y.M.C.A., where he was staying. The lobby was well filled with men when the hour arrived, but it was not hard to distinguish him in the crowd. After introductions, we went into one of the offices at the side of the lobby and sat down to talk, and in five minutes he was addressing me as "Miss Louise." So entirely devoid of pomposity and so thoroughly approachable was he that the embarrassment and awe I had feared were forgotten entirely. Perhaps it was not so much the humility of the man as his *simplicity* that put me so readily at ease. The humility was undoubtedly there but so sincere, so really a part of the man was it that it did not protrude as dissimulated forms of that grace might have done. To a stranger who had never heard of his books or the homage paid him as an author, there seemed to have been no reason why he should *not* be humble. The impression he gave was that of a quiet, meditative man, of gentle, kindly spirit, easily approachable, and without any consciousness of superiority.

The Braille idea was new to him; he had never had any special contact with the blind and did not know of the scarcity of evangelical literature in embossed type and the wide-spread circulation of Catholic, Russellite, Seventh Day Adventist, Christian Science, and Theosophist publications. Nor did he realize that there were a hundred thousand blind persons in this country alone. He was profoundly impressed by these facts, and asked to have a written statement of them that he might present to a Richmond friend who would doubtless be interested. Prior to this, I had no thought of any other plan than that his books should be put into Braille, and sent out from the Silver Publishing Society office in Pittsburgh; but as we talked on, he said, "You know if the Lord should see fit to initiate a work of this kind for the blind, He might have a

very definite part in it for you—it might have its
base right here in Richmond. At any rate, let's pray
for His guidance. If He wants it, He will surely furnish
the necessary funds without solicitation on our part.
The circulation of my printed books has been kept up
for about thirty years (Mr. Kelker's work began about
1895) by means of voluntary offerings, so I think we
are safe to conclude that He will send offerings sufficient to make a start, if He wants this undertaken.
Meantime, let's pray about it and mention the matter
to friends as we are led."

There were many more interviews that winter and
early spring regarding the proposition with the result
that the friend to whom he had referred gave Mr.
McConkey a check for fifty dollars. Mr. McConkey
himself gave fifty, and this was followed by another
gift of fifty and several smaller ones. He turned over
the little treasury to me, and we placed our order with
a Braille printing house for two hundred copies of
Chastening, which were to be sent out as gifts to any
who accepted the offer we were making through a
secular Braille magazine. The books were received so
gladly by blind readers in various parts of the country
that it seemed wise to depart from the original plan
of sending them out as gifts and send them instead
as loans. So later in the year, the Braille Circulating
Library was duly established with headquarters in a
closet in my room! But no one needed to see it as
the work was all done by mail and, after all, the virtue
of a library does not lie in its situation! The nucleus
consisted of forty copies each of *Faith*, *The Fifth
Sparrow*, and *The God Planned Life*, besides some
reprints of *Chastening*. From the very first, there

was a live response from readers, and many letters proving that vital spiritual blessing was being received from them.

In those early days, I said something to him about my appreciation of his trusting me to use wisely the funds turned over to me, and he said, "Why, I would trust you with the last cent I had!" It is not hard to imagine the thrill those words produced in the heart of such a young, weak, untaught member of the Body. This willingness to place perfect confidence in his weaker brethren was perhaps the thing that endeared him most to them.

It was interesting to watch and see how he would bear testimony. If ever a man ministered the Spirit, he did. One could hardly ride on the same elevator with him and not feel the presence of God, though he might not say a word. Fifteen minutes spent in fellowship with him was like a breath from heaven. He never stayed in any company long without giving a verbal testimony. I recall one evening Mr. McConkey called on me and found others present who were not particularly interested in Christian literature for the blind. Although they were church members they rarely had heard, much less given testimony for the Lord. I wondered how Mr. McConkey would get in a word for the Lord Jesus. While I was wondering, no doubt he was praying as Nehemiah did, for wisdom. Then someone asked a polite question about Mr. McConkey's early life, and this gave him an opportunity to tell something of his financial struggles and responsibilities, concluding by saying: "The man who afterward became my brother-in-law, and whom I always call 'D.S.', was at that time president of the bank in

Wrightsville. When in after years, we talked of those crucial times, when my note was passed around the table, he would tell me how the board of directors would shake their heads and say, 'He'll never pull through.' But the Lord brought me through and I was able to make all the note good." This led to further opportunities for giving God the praise. It was always thus. His conversations usually began with a remark as casual as the opening sentence to the woman at the well, but invariably some spiritual gift was imparted before the end. He once remarked that wherever Andrew was seen in the Scriptures he was always bringing someone to the Lord Jesus. So it was with James of the twentieth century.

It was, of course, this complete dependence on God and the use of prayer as a means of bringing forth God's power which caused him constantly to practice that injunction, "In *everything* by prayer . . ." One of the first things he did after the Braille work was launched was to write me as follows:

"I am now suggesting that we form a prayer council of friends in Richmond composed of the following names: Mr. Robert Friend, Mr. Wade McCargo, Mr. Brown, and Mr. Buchanan, secretary of the Y.M.C.A. You might either write or see these friends. Ask them for me if they would join such a little prayer council. All we would expect of them would be to meet with you some day at the Y.M.C.A., perhaps about the noon hour. You can tell them that our work is launched and have them join with you in prayer for God's blessing on it. . . . I would like to write each one in person, but am tired and pressed with other work. . . . These friends are all busy men, and I would not expect them to have a regular date for the prayer service but simply come together as you might call them for any special emergency in the work, also to hold up the work in prayer in their own private devotions."

Mr. Wade McCargo, mentioned in the letter, and his wife, a young married couple who lived in a three-room apartment in South Richmond, were also newly born into the kingdom, and hungry for the sincere milk of the Word. They loved to have Mr. McConkey in their home, and he often rode across the city on a street car to be with them and to share some spiritual truth. They invited him to meals, and although he could eat very little, he accepted. After the meal, there was, as his hostess expressed it, "a feast of truth."

Later, as Mr. McCargo's business grew, they were able to have a car and an attractive bungalow of their own; and it was their delight to drive to town for Mr. McConkey and have him enjoy the comforts of their new home. But they never forgot that he had been the same gracious friend in their early married life as in the more prosperous times that followed. No one rejoiced for their sakes more than he because of their prosperity, but as far as he himself was concerned no one cared less whether his friends were rich or poor. He had the rare grace of enjoying with others the gifts they had received from God.

These associations had, first of all, the glow of the human, for James McConkey loved people for their own sake. A family visit was far from a common-place event; he held their joys and sorrows in common with them. But if this had been all, Christendom would never have received from his pen those pages that have caused hearts to glow and lives to burn out for Christ in all parts of the world. But this was not all for every contact was touched with the Divine. The purpose of each conversation was not to expound some theological truth, but rather to have a sweet savor of Christ. He had learned shortly after his surrender that the *kind* of task made no difference provided it was the one assigned by the Master Workman. He was as content to sit in a family group and talk informally as to address hundreds from a platform. His theme was the same in both cases, and he had no more responsibility for results, so why should numbers matter?

Such contacts were having a great deal to do with the making of his books. There ought to be no compulsion laid on men to set forth the tremendous facts of human life for others to read unless they understand human beings and know how to appeal to them. Through personal experience, he learned to count heart-throbs. He saw others suffering disappointment, as he himself had, and by getting close to them he learned how best to present the one Cure for all heartaches. His books and pamphlets written out of his own experience of suffering went straight into other suffering hearts! Humanly speaking, it was this kinship with suffering ones that set his books going—his interpretation of human need and Divine sufficiency. He wrote *to* the average Christian *for the purpose* of making him *above* the average; he took people where he found them— lukewarm—and sought, by the Spirit, to bring them to white heat.

When he taught about prayer, he began with beginners, but encouraged them each step of the way. Above everything he urged that they *pray*, whether they knew how or not! He reminded them that while they took time to hold the promises before God, He would act: things would move: no time would be lost by praying. And so he led men on from this elementary conception of prayer to its highest form, that of communion. They might have been very indifferent sort of Christians in the beginning but they had come to realize that prayer was a practical matter about which this man was qualified to teach them. However, it was not the practicalness of his book on prayer which caused it to grip people, but it was the sympathetic attitude of the author. The reader sensed in every paragraph that back of it all was an all-consuming love for God and its necessary by-product, an all-considerate love for men. And it is not hard to learn from a teacher who loves you.

The beginning of the Braille Library was about the time of the inception of the Richmond Bible Conference Association, which came about in the same small, quiet way. Since he had been used for years in this type of work, it was natural that he should begin thinking of the possibility of having regular conferences in Richmond. The City was highly denominationalized, and the idea of an inter-denominational organization of this kind was not acceptable to many of the religious leaders. But there were enough who saw the need to make a nucleus, so he talked the matter over with them. As a result, he met with this group of ministers and laymen (women were not admitted to the executive board until later) in the Y.M.C.A., and plans were made for an association which would have as its purpose the bringing of spiritual leaders to Richmond for the purpose of Bible teaching. The only qualification for membership was the signing of a statement of faith which was in accord with the teaching of all evangelical denominations. This, of course, debarred some who really gave the matter serious thought, who had been too strongly influenced by Modernistic teachers and periodicals. Others who had no objection to the degree of orthodoxy required, saw no need of anything outside their own denominational enterprises. Why bring these Bible teachers to Richmond when all the denominations here had good preachers? Why not go to your own church and hear the Bible expounded instead of hearing it by means of such a mixed-up group? So their policy was hands off. But there was a small group, as in Pittsburgh and other places, who were eager to hear dispensational truth, to know more about prophecy, and somehow to get the deeper things not fully set forth in the average church. It was this group that supported him in forming the organization.

Mr. McConkey himself did very little speaking in the conferences as his strength would not permit so many engagements, but he was the guiding spirit of it all through those early years. Some of the first speakers, who were also warm friends of his, were Dr. George Guille, Canon F. E. Howitt, and Dr. Robert C. McQuilkin. Thus, in a city where a sermon on the impending coming of the Lord and the rapture of the saints was almost an unheard-of thing, began the teaching of prophecy and the emphasizing of the essential truths of Christianity.

This was ever his method of defeating Modernism, just to give those blessed truths in the power of the Spirit and to trust that same Spirit to give discernment to hearers so that thereafter they would not be satisfied with froth or subtle error. In his public messages he did not spend much time in dealing with Modernistic views or personalities. One Sunday morning in speaking before a group whose pastor appeared to be the middle-of-the-road type, if not a decided Liberal, he said, "A very distinguished preacher somewhat after the modern order said, a couple of years ago, that Jesus Christ came to reveal the hidden splendors in the human soul, and I turned, as he told it, to the fifth chapter of Galatians to notice God's picture of the human soul, and here it is: *"Now the works of the flesh are manifest, which are these, adultery, fornication, uncleanness, lasciviousness; idolatry, witchcraft, hatred, variance, emulations, wrath, strife, seditions, heresies; envyings, murders, drunkenness, revelings and such like."*

"If that is the soul of hidden splendors that Jesus Christ came to reveal, it would be an unfortunate day for you and me. No, 'in me, that is in my flesh, dwelleth no good thing' and any earnest soul knows that the only hidden splendor in our natural, human hearts is that of Colossians 1: 27, 'Christ in you the hope of glory'."

He did not call the name of the "distinguished preacher," but doubtless the pastor and a few others in the group knew to whom he referred.

But while he did not publicly denounce the pronounced Liberals by name, his teaching was always diametrically opposed to theirs and he never failed to let the public know where he stood in matters of doctrine. His public associations were altogether with those who stood firmly for the Word so none could ever say, "Undoubtedly, Mr. McConkey himself is sound but why does he seem to enjoy fellowship with Liberals?"

But while his public ministry was spent in constructive teaching, rather than in destructive criticism, he never failed to express himself in private when asked his opinion in regard to various outstanding Liberals and their teaching. During a discussion, a young lady asked him one day, "But, Mr. McConkey, isn't there such a thing as a Christian's accepting Darwin's theory of evolution?" "I don't see how there could be," he answered, and straightway she changed the course of her reading. Perhaps the brevity of his answers helped to make them convincing, but whatever it was, she felt that this man knew what he was talking about—that the time she had been spending on Modernistic reading had been worse than wasted.

One day as he was arranging for a meeting of a certain group at the "Y", someone remarked that one o'clock would not do as that was the hour for the noon-day service at ———— Church. Now the speakers at these meetings were some of the most outstanding Liberals of the North but this friend did not yet have discernment enough to know it, although she had been receiving, according to her capacity, all the truth Mr. McConkey had been giving her. He did not reprove her but simply said, "I didn't think the members of our group would be planning to go there." It was enough. The friend began to think, to compare the addresses of these men with the burden of the Bible, and the noon-day meetings were minus her presence. If he had reprimanded her sharply, the result might have been quite different.

X

IN ALL THINGS, CHARITY !

As THE Braille Library grew and speaking engagements became more numerous, he found himself more
and more attached to Richmond and his stay each year
grew longer. The reason he was acceptable to so many
types of pastors in the city is explained by that happy
balance of grace and truth of which he had written
and which they had seen exemplified in his life. Some
of the men who invited him to their pulpits would have
looked with disfavor on certain Bible teachers who
doubtless taught as much truth as he, but did not mix
it with as much grace. These ministers might not have
been able to discern subtle errors in Liberal teachers
nor define the exact difference between their theology
and Mr. McConkey's, but they loved the man and they
knew he drew them right into the presence of God,
so they sought him. It was with this class that his
best work was done. Those who espoused an ultra-
liberal theology did not want his message. The well-
taught, consecrated Christians were not so desperately
in need of it, but the babes in Christ, the untaught,
were in the balance, and it was his purpose to buy up
these opportunities for the Lord.

He never went into the pulpit without a period of
prayer immediately preceding. For this reason it was

never his policy to speak to a Bible class and then go immediately into church service. He always arrived at the church early and spent half an hour alone in prayer in the pastor's study. Then when preliminaries were almost over, his friends would watch for the tall form to cross quietly into his place. He had no gestures, no trick of speaking. While at times there was an awkwardness in his posture, he never moved about in the pulpit or practiced the nervous mannerisms of certain public speakers. If this piece of clay was slightly awkward it was of no consequence compared with the holy use the Lord was making of it.

At first the observer saw only a man of mediocre appearance, with iron-gray hair and mustache, with a serious expression around the mouth, and with deep blue eyes that spoke of chastening and of charity. He heard a moderately deep voice in a conversational tone, earnestly, lovingly stating his premises. Then gradually, the speaker faded out entirely; the message so quietly given was taken up, as it were, by a great spiritual amplifier. It did not stop in the head but kept on to the heart; men and women went out, not the same. And the secret of it all was expressed, perhaps most concisely, in the "Jottings" quoted in Chapter Two. It was not due solely to half an hour's prayer previous to the time of the message, but primarily because the life that day and days before had been measured alongside the Book. The test of each word and act was whether it had been prompted by the Spirit. It was this moment-by-moment abiding before the message was given that made it so acceptable to those who hungered and thirsted for righteousness.

His addresses were sometimes what he called "teaching messages," and sometimes devotional messages; but whichever they were, he was careful not to antagonize, unless an earnest presentation of truth delivered in a constructive way would create antagonism. He always spoke the truth in love, but more than that, he delivered it with such lucid logic and penetrating clarity that a wealth of illumination was shed upon the gospel's sacred page. Even an untutored wayfarer experienced a spiritual illumination by the simplicity and directness of the speaker's appeal. There were certain great spiritual principles that Mr. McConkey emphasized. His first thought was the yielding of the life. Out of great tribulation he had learned the importance of this step, and his heart burned within him as he endeavored to unfold to his listeners the power and beauty of a life wholly dedicated to God. He felt reasonably sure that Spirit-directed Bible study would follow such a decision and with it an increasing ability to handle aright the Word of Truth. The richness of his spiritual experience is nowhere better revealed than in his tract, *The Dedicated Life*. When he exhorts his hearers to "Give your life to God, and God will fill your life," he knows full well what the Lord has done for his soul, and he wants every other man to enter into the same rich experience. To make his meaning crystal clear on this point he uses in another tract an illustration in which there is a wealth of meaning:

"I was standing on the wall of a great lock. Outside was a huge lake vessel about to enter. At my feet lay the empty lock—waiting. For what? Waiting to be filled. Away beyond lay great Lake Superior with its limitless abundance of supply, also waiting. Waiting for what? Waiting for something to be done at the lock ere the great lake could pour in its fullness. In a moment it was done. The lock-keeper reached out his hand and touched a steel lever. A little wicket gate sprang open under the magic touch. At once the water in the lock began to boil, and seethe. As it did so I saw it rapidly creeping up the walls of the lock. In a few moments the lock was full. The great gates swung open and the huge ship floated into the lock now filled to the brim with the fullness inpoured from the waiting lake without.

"Is not this a picture of a great truth about the Holy Spirit? Here are God's children, like that empty lock, waiting to be filled. And, as the great inland sea outside the lock was willing and waiting to pour its abundance into the lock, so here is God willing to pour His fullness of life into the lives of His children. But He is waiting. For what? Waiting as the lake waited, for something to be done by us. Waiting for us to reach forth and touch that tiny wicket gate of consecration through which His abundant life shall flow and fill. Is it hard to move? Does the rust of worldliness corrode it? Do the weeds and ivy-vines of selfishness cling about it and choke it? Is the will stubborn, and slow to yield? Yet God is waiting for it. And once it is done He reveals Himself in fullness of life even as He has promised; even as He has been all the time willing and ready to do. For all the barriers and hindrances have been upon our side; not upon His. They are the barriers, not of His unwillingness but of our unyieldedness. And do you say you got all of Christ when you were saved? Doubtless you did, but the point in issue here is not whether you got all of Christ, but did Christ get all of you?"

But let no one think he escaped criticism entirely. There were some who objected to the high plane of Christian living he preached. In spite of the tact and winsomeness and yearning love that surrounded every message, God's Word is still sharper than any two-edged sword and the call of separation from the world has never been a welcome one to the masses. The saying is too hard for them. Some of them were counted orthodox and highly disapproved of an easy-going Christianity in any form, but this idea of giving one's life unreservedly to the Lord was not such a comfortable doctrine and then, too, it might border on fanaticism! Some said that if Mr. McConkey didn't take care, he would be classed with the "perfectionists." One woman objected strongly to his books because, she said, they were "too much like sanctification," meaning the particular doctrine held by some who taught sanctification as a "second blessing" and perfection as a present attainment.

On the heels of this protest came one from Mr. X, a minister, who took him to task because he had stated definitely in his first book that the Holy Spirit indwelt every believer, that He came in at conversion and that His coming was not a *second* blessing. This man of zeal who approved Mr. McConkey's teaching in many other respects called on him at the Y.M.C.A. for the purpose of enlightening him. Concerning the interview, Mr. McConkey said, "I did something I seldom allow myself to do and that was to get into an argument with him." It ended as most arguments do, with each party unmoved in his conviction.

During the winters from 1925 to 1929, Mr. McConkey's main work in Richmond was "giving messages" (he never spoke of it as preaching) in the various churches, chiefly among the Presbyterian, Baptist, Episcopal, and Methodist. He had long made it a practice to try out his written messages in this way; it helped him, he said, to get the reaction of the audience. Usually, his message was one of the new ones that had not yet appeared in print, but occasionally he gave an old one. On one occasion he even consented to give a talk on his life and work at the Union Theological Seminary, in Richmond.

Several friends had anticipated getting an insight into his early personal life at this time, but they were disappointed. Everything in that address was built around the work to which he had been called. A man who refused to allow the story of his life to be written during his earthly pilgrimage, certainly would not spend much time talking about his experiences and characteristics. No, the characteristics were ignored altogether and only such experiences as touched his life-work were mentioned. The theme of it all was the Lord's gracious guidance in initiating and establishing the Silver Publishing Society. The instrument He had used for this purpose was either ignored or carefully kept in the background. If any had expected a skilfully disguised eulogy on the man, they went away disappointed. To God was all the glory!

I recall he was invited to speak at a Bible conference in one of the Episcopal churches, and later, in commenting upon it to a friend, he remarked, "Mr. Reed said it was not at all necessary to wear the vestments and, Miss H, I didn't even change my blue tie." He was possessed of dignity on every occasion but he had a natural revulsion to formalism, to anything that might have a tendency to freeze the heart out of Christianity.

After speaking at Trinity Methodist church on "God's Jewel Case," emphasizing the believer's safety in Christ, he used somewhat the same theme at Christ Episcopal Church. Both congregations, of course, were composed of members of the Arminian persuasion who would have expressed decided opposition to purely Calvinistic theology, but when the doctrine of the security of the believer was clothed so Scripturally and presented so appealingly, it was not hard to accept. One member was so delighted at the presentation of "No Condemnation," that she said afterwards it was the only time in her life she had felt like shouting. The message had never appeared in print so it was new to all. Even to those who were already well grounded in the teaching there were new revelations and fresh illustrations of the way God keeps those who have come to Him through His Son.

The gift of being lovingly uncompromising was peculiarly his. People who would have looked askance at predestination preached as such would swallow *The God-Planned Life* whole, and those who considered the security of the believer a deadly doctrine, sure to breed laxity in the Christian life, were enthusiastic about *No Condemnation*. There were various contributing causes for this. One was that every thought, even in the printed messages, was couched in gentle terms, between the lines there was always respect, and consideration for the reader. In the oral messages there was added to this, vocal inflection that bespoke loving sympathy and understanding for the hearer. Pupil and teacher were made to feel themselves on one plane, with the Holy Spirit as the teacher of both. It is easy enough to compromise the truth in order to avoid offense, or to speak out so dogmatically that the hearer is palpably irritated, but the happy combination of loyalty to the Word of God and speaking the truth with loving understanding of the flock is rare.

This spirit of brotherly consideration reached its climax at a union service in one of the suburban churches where Mr. McConkey was the speaker on a Wednesday evening. All pastors of the churches represented had a part in the preliminaries. When the time for Scripture reading (II Samuel 9) came, the minister to whom this had been assigned evidently did not possess a self-pronouncing Bible. Through the whole passage he insisted on pronouncing Mephibosheth's name as if it had been Me-phi-bo'-sheth, bearing down hard on the third syllable. Knowing Mr. McConkey as I did, I wondered how he could avoid an implied correction of his brother in Christ when he began to speak on the son of Jonathan. So passionately did he love accuracy, he could hardly be expected to follow the example of the royal lady who drank out of her own finger-bowl after seeing that her less-privileged guest had mistaken its purpose. And yet so scrupulous was he in considering the feelings of others that it was difficult to picture him following this speaker and using the correct pronunciation of the word at every turn. He had announced the title of the message as "Lame Feet," that its purpose was to show Mephibosheth as a type of sinner, saved, and now enjoying the grace of God, through the merit of His Son. Consequently we knew something of what was to come. We listened intently, not only to get the truth but to see how he would solve the problem that had presented itself. We began to wonder when he would meet the issue, would come out and pronounce the name. First, it was "the grandson of Saul," then "the lame man," then "the son of Jonathan"—and thus it continued! Toward the close of the message we realized, of course, that this was done deliberately, in order to avoid pronouncing the name at all. But the message went over!

When he came into the office the next day, he said, "A strange thing happened last night—" And when I met him with a knowing smile, he said, "Oh, you're entirely too canny. I must admit I was nonplussed. I had never thought of his mispronouncing the name, but when he did, I simply sent up a prayer for guidance and all through the message, the Lord gave me substitutes to use for Mephibosheth's name and gave them in such a way that there was no awkwardness in avoiding the name itself."

And there had been no awkwardness whatever. Doubtless no one in the audience guessed that an adjustment had had to be made in the pulpit, except those who had heard him speak of it informally before. They may have forgotten the Scripture taught in LAME FEET but it is safe to say they have not forgotten the speaker's application of the law of love.

One beautiful, crisp Sunday morning in Westminster Presbyterian Church, he gave *God Given Men* for the first time in Richmond. As he brought home in that gently impressive way of his the great truth that each of us has his own circle of God-given men to reach, that we, insignificant as we may seem, are better fitted

for that specific task than anyone else in the world,
a young lady in the congregation began to get a vision
of practical evangelism. That afternoon as she went
to the City Jail for personal work among the women
there, she prayed that she might be directed to her
God-given woman and she was! It happened that the
Lord led her to a young girl of nineteen, committed
to reform school when her trial came up. This Christian worker had many helpful associations from time
to time with the girl in the jail, and this unfortunate
one always stood out in the mind of the Christian
worker as the first of her "God-given women."

He summed up his method of teaching in three
words: "State, illustrate, apply," and it was this practical application which always came last that did the
work. No earnest soul could sit under one of his messages and not be stirred to do, or give or yield!

In one of his tracts, *The God-Planned Life*, Mr.
McConkey restates this same truth with beautiful and
convincing clarity:

"There is no man in all the world who can do your
work as well as you. And if you do not find and enter
into God's purpose for your life, there will be something missing from the glory that would otherwise have
been there. Every jewel gleams with its own radiance.
Every flower distils its own fragrance. Every Christian
has his own particular bit of Christ's radiance and
Christ's fragrance which God would pass through him
to others. Has God given you a particular personality?
He has also created a particular circle of individuals
who can be reached and touched by that personality
as by none other in the wide world. And then He
shapes and orders your life so as to bring you into

contact with that very circle. Just a hair's breadth of shift in the focus of the telescope, and some man sees a vision of beauty which before had been all confused and befogged. So, too, just that grain of individual and personal variation in your life from every other man's and some one sees Jesus Christ with a clearness and beauty he would discern nowhere else. What a joy to know that God will use it, as He uses no other for certain individuals susceptible to it as to no other! In you there is just a bit of change in the angle of the jewel and lo, some man sees the light! In you there is just a trifle of variation in the mingling of the species—and, behold, some one becomes conscious of the fragrance of Christ."

Of all the messages I have ever heard him give, *The Dedicated Life* impressed me most. Although I had read it over and over in print, there was something new in it when given orally by the man who had lived it out long before putting it on paper. The time was a Sunday evening in Mizpah Church. There was a reverent hush over the congregation as he read of the burnt offering from the first chapter of Leviticus. After the message, he did a thing that was rare with him; he asked the audience for a response. As they sat with bowed heads, he asked those who had dedicated their lives to the Lord before coming in, or would do it that moment to say quietly with him, "Lord, I have done it." There was never any place for humor in his messages. One could hardly imagine a witticism being mingled with so much solemn truth. Those who expected anything of the kind went away disappointed. But there was always an atmosphere of vital sympathy, of "getting under the load," and the very tone of his voice conveyed comfort and hope to his hearers.

The next day one friend who had been present said to him, "Mr. McConkey, there were tears in my eyes most of the time when you were speaking last night." He answered, "Howard (Banks) says the same thing was true when he heard that message. But it was an old one for you," he added, apologetically.

Mr. Banks once said that soon after he came into possession of certain great truths concerning prophecy and the victorious life, he became extremely critical of all who did not say his Shibboleth. He had a certain pride, which he considered justifiable, in his ability to discern error and spiritual faults, and he did not fail to express his findings to Mr. McConkey. One Sunday they had listened to the same visiting preacher, who was not Modernistic by any means, but who lacked some of the qualities this enthusiastic young Christian thought a minister of the Gospel should have. Mr. Banks was well-nigh bursting with the satisfaction of having a logical and just criticism to give forth when he was completely disarmed by the suave statement from Mr. McConkey: "You know, Howard, I think Dr. ——— is one of the greatest pulpiteers of his generation." "It cured me," said Mr. Banks. "His treatment was much more effective than my own medicine—criticism."

This did not mean that he would have passed over the Dr. ——— incident if there had been a trace of Modernism in his utterances, but in those days, in the South, there was not a great deal of heterodoxy in the pulpits. Doubtless there was plenty of powerless preaching, which was nevertheless orthodox, but about

this he would never express himself. If a man
preached sound doctrine, there was nothing for him to
say; he would not condemn the lack of power in the
lives of fellow-Christians.

Modernists are constantly making gibes at the chilly
orthodoxy of Fundamentalists, and Fundamentalists, in
turn, have assumed an attitude that might easily pro-
voke such remarks. Occasionally, for instance, one is
found who, instead of showing the fallacies of Christian Science and its diametrical opposition to the
Gospel and leaving the matter there, will go off into
fierce denunciation of Mrs. Eddy and wax witty about
the number of her marriages. But it was not in Mr.
McConkey's nature to make fun of anyone nor was
there anything in Christian Science or any other un-
scriptural cult to stir his sense of humor. It was too
tragic altogether. He once said in speaking of a ministerial friend, "Yes, we're good friends. The only time
we disagree is when he begins to tell jokes." His
policy was never to denounce or ridicule personalities,
but to expose fallacies by constructive teaching. It
was the best method he knew to prove that he loved
the sinner even though he hated the sin. If there were
those in his audience who criticized his position, at
least they would appreciate his courtesy and might
hear him again. Above all, they must have no grounds
for accusing him of uncharitableness, for this would
dishonor the Lord and His cause.

As far as one could see, the system worked. Modernists, as a rule, let him alone. I have never heard of
one who had a personal dislike for him. Sometimes
they attacked his books, as Thomas Lomax Hunter,
columnist for the *Times Dispatch* (a Richmond news-

paper) did *The End Of The Age*, but he never took up these matters for discussion. His time and strength were kept for giving more messages of the same kind rather than defending those already put forth. He and Mr. Banks shared the view that dealing with apostate Christianity was a well-nigh hopeless task that was not worth the effort.

His fellowship, of course, was in the body of Christ, and truly he had fellowship with some of the weakest and most untaught members. These untutored men knew very little theology, but they accepted the Bible as the Word of God and the blood of Christ as the only means of salvation. That was enough. It was natural that he should derive more enjoyment from fellowship with theologians, because there was a commonalty of interest for the deeper things. But these professional expositors of religion were treated with not a scintilla more of respect than the weak and ignorrant. He was a thorough-going Calvinist in his convictions, but some of the most loyal of his spiritual friends were Arminians, men who would not have stood for Calvinism under any circumstances but who seemed to agree with whatever Mr. McConkey taught. I remember the smile that lurked around his mouth when he learned how one of these who so decidedly opposed predestination had "simply swallowed *The God Planned Life whole!*" But he made it a point never to discuss non-essentials. Such things as modes of baptism were absorbed in the all-important theme of consecration. All that counted with him was a man's surrender to God, a surrender complete enough to transcend denominational differences.

Strong though he was for the premillennial coming

of Christ, he handled this subject with care, presenting it to believers whose confidence he had in some measure won, and showing them step by step how it was not only taught but emphasized all through the Bible. Never did he upbraid them because they were slow of heart to comprehend his teaching on the subject. Nor was he critical of their denominational leaders who either taught post-millennialism or ignored the subject altogether. There was always this circle: if believers yielded their lives to the Lord, they would love His Word; if they loved it, they would study it; and under the guidance of the Holy Spirit, they would learn what He wanted them to know about the second coming. So he won adherents to this doctrine as to all others by means of love. This does not mean that he ever hesitated to cry out against sin and false teaching, but he did it in an impersonal way and trusted the Holy Spirit to send conviction where it belonged. He realized that no amount of vituperation could convict a soul—that the Holy Spirit must do this in His own way, and His way through His servant, James, was always a quiet, gentle one.

XI

A YOKEFELLOW — NOT A DOGMATIST

SOMETIMES there were protests from Pittsburgh directed against the speaking activities of Mr. McConkey because his friends in the office knew all too well the danger of overwork. It is easy to imagine his reluctance to refuse pastors who so sincerely desired his services and who themselves had no physical handicap. A pastor of one of the suburban churches came one day to the Braille Library to invite him to speak in the church on any date he would suggest. Mr. McConkey had gone out, but I told the gentleman I was afraid there was no chance of his giving a favorable response as he had said that very day that he must not make another engagement for fear of seriously overtaxing his strength. The pastor turned away sorrowfully, and said, "I've been trying to get that man into my church for fifteen years!" This was quoted to Mr. McConkey and he relented.

Every kindness shown him was always repaid in good measure, pressed down, and running over. It was useless to remonstrate. One summer during vacation he did a favor for me which was so undeserved he must have known I should hesitate to accept it, so he wrote:

"Don't say me nay, now, Timothea, for my heart is set on it and I can do so little to show my appreciation of your loving service to our common Lord.

149

"I trust you have a lovely vacation. I am praying about the matters you mentioned in your letter to me. Our Father will work them all out in His own wondrous way. Am getting a splendid rest for awhile for which I am so grateful to Him. The head is much better. Almost passed the sawdust stage!!!

"It is very lovely in you to acquiesce so graciously in my suggestion about *The God Planned Life*. I am most grateful to the Lord that He has given me a fellow-worker who is so willing and so ready to defer to another's judgment in these matters. Not many people have that lovely grace of yieldedness which you possess so aboundingly."

Each association with him as chief was a revelation of his humility. These intimate contacts afforded us opportunities to see the working of his soul at close range. Here was a man who might have attained a high place of power and influence in the world of affairs, but was perfectly content to live and move among lowly people, without a thought of worldly applause. In his own eyes he was never anything but a servant, a bond-slave of *Jesus Christ*! When he pronounced that name, whether publicly or privately, there was something in his tone of voice that inspired awe, reverence, worship, obedience! The major concern of his life was to find out what Jesus Christ had laid out for him that day and then to do it. Service not in line with obedience to the Master was not worthy of the name. It made no difference whether he was writing a book that would thrill thousands, whether he was discussing some small detail of business policy or whether he was talking to a child about Jesus. The only thing that did matter was the command of the Lord. Doubtless it was this consciousness of servant-ship that made him so approachable. In his private intervals he invariably revealed his utter dependence upon His Master. He claimed no ability to write or speak with power except under the guidance and direction of the Holy Spirit.

He listened to suggestions from his subordinates as if they had been mandates from Solomon, and whenever possible, accepted their proposals with consummate graciousness. He never made them feel that they had proposed some foolish plan. He used psychology, Christian psychology, at every turn, methods by which any business man might profit. The result was a rock-ribbed loyalty, not only from those officially connected with him in Pittsburgh and in Richmond, but from unofficial friends who often discussed with him the best way to carry on his work. He might have written volumes on psychology, if strength had permitted, but he chose rather to teach only two basic principles of living, faith toward God and love toward men.

It was this recognition of the reality of Christ, of His headship in the work of distributing the printed page which explains the phenomenal growth of the Silver Publishing Society and the Braille Circulating Library. The Lord has given His promise to honor those who honor Him, and the fulfillment of these promises was seen every day in these offices. Nothing aside from the daily routine was done without first seeking to learn the mind of the Lord in the matter. If the mail brought suggestions of ways in which the work might be enlarged, or curtailed, they were tabled until the whole thing could be spread before the Lord. Never a day passed in the Pittsburgh office without definite offering of prayer for the work. As the little group knelt in the inner office, there was a conviction in each heart that the Lord was ruling there, that Mr. McConkey was only a fellow-servant with them, yet a servant who always had a clearer understanding of the Master's will than any of the rest.

At first we had no set rules for united prayer. The work of the Braille Library was in its beginnings, and the problems were not complicated. Whenever a difficult situation arose, he and I prayed together about it. There was never anything mechanical about his religious devotions. Apparently every thought of his had been brought into captivity and so it was as natural as breathing for him to talk about the Lord, to pray, or to expound a Scriptural passage. Anything that touched the glory of God was breath of life to him, and anything that did not was a secondary matter.

He made no rules for others regarding their prayer-life (or anything else) but he was strict in regard to his own. Perhaps one reason why the Lord allowed the nerve-condition to remain that prohibited more than twenty or thirty minutes a day of writing was the opportunity it gave for longer periods of prayer. It might be safe to conclude that if all the Christian literature released by the press had revealed work and prayer in the proportion given to his books, the results would be amazingly different. It was not that his books had a much wider circulation than those of many other Christian authors, but the astonishing thing is that they achieved results that were absolutely beyond computation when measured by human standards. Although he could not write much he could pray much! There were definite times to meet the Lord each day when his soul was poured out for the assimilation of the messages, for the support of the work, for the receiving of new messages. His book on prayer was written out of experiences that had been burned into his soul; he had learned years ago that it was the fundamental function of the spirit.

Because this was true his first thought in promoting any project was to form a prayer group for it. He never complained about lack of coöperation from the Christian people but he did remark one day in the office as we were talking about a prayer group: "It's harder to get people to pray than to do anything else in the world. They will give money or service or anything more easily than time to prayer." He would call on us raw recruits to pray with him about fine points in the work as if we had been veterans. At one time, there was an acute situation in Pittsburgh, involving personalities, which was heavy on his heart. It was necessary for him to go into a detailed description of the matter before we could pray intelligently about it. We could not fail to see the expression of real hurt in the gray-blue eyes as he mentioned several facts which might have implied criticism of his friends. No one who saw him and heard his tones could ever think there was even a suggestion of relish in the relating of these facts. The indelible impression left upon us was that he considered us worthy to enter into this fellowship of prayer with him.

It is impossible to separate the man from the message. His messages were himself. While he was able to comfort a few of the sin-sick and heartbroken who came to him personally, he counted on his books to perform a similar and more extended ministry in the remote corners of the earth. A widow, once heartbroken but now heart-healed, wrote from Brazil to say how the friendly hand had been extended across continents and had carried to her the books that had meant balm to her soul. Silver and gold she had none, but to show her appreciation she had translated seven of the tracts into Portuguese and was waiting for the way to be opened for their publication.

It was his appraisal of others that invariably served as an index to his character. He had a logical mind, developed by legal training which could not forbear analyses, but every judgment was so tempered with mercy that one sometimes wondered whether or not he really saw people clearly. For instance, I was asking him to describe a certain friend and he spoke in this way: "Well, G is rather short, has pretty good weight, blue eyes, and a very gentle, deferential manner." Later, after I had met G——, I recognized the gentle, deferential manner all right but it could not altogether hide from my less charitable eyes the fact that he was one of the most unattractive *looking* men one could imagine. "There's no art to find the mind's construction in the face," nor is it charitable to pass final judgment on a man by a casual reading of his countenance. A life controlled by the spirit of love, such as Mr. McConkey's could not speak ill of his brother.

An eminent Englishman has said that thoughtfulness for others, generosity, modesty, and self-respect, are the qualities which make a real gentleman as distinguished from the veneered article which commonly goes by that name. In his attitude toward women he admirably exemplified this definition of a gentleman. A blind girl who was bright and interesting, but decidedly mediocre in appearance came into the office one day and spent a short time in friendly visitation. After her departure, Mr. McConkey turned to me and said, "I declare that's a beautiful face," without realizing that the only beauty it possessed was the radiance that love had thrown upon it. This was characteristic of his charity toward women, and served to emphasize the qualities that marked him as a princely Christian.

It seemed to give him actual pain when some fellow-Christian failed God. We were speaking one day of a religious organization that enrolled among its workers a woman who was evidently not suited to the position. Although she was no special friend of his, it was easy to see how her attitude toward her work hurt him. Finally he said, "Well, we can only pray that the Lord will either transform her or transfer her!"

In his offices in both Pittsburgh and Richmond, it never seemed to occur to him that his dear yokefellows would neglect the work any more than he would. When I came on in 1929 as a full-time worker in the Braille Library, he said, "Now you just manage things to suit yourself. If you want to go out of town for a day or two for something special, just close the office and go ahead. And, of course, don't hesitate to stay at home if you are not feeling well. You know the situation. I'm leaving the whole thing in your hands."

Oh, the unconscious psychology of it! Who wouldn't work under a man like that? No wonder Mr. Banks and Mr. Lane and Mr. Gardner (the two secretaries who followed Mr. Banks) adored him! To him they were "Howard" and "Morty" and "Frank"—younger brothers but yet fellow-servants whose judgment in all matters was treated with the utmost respect. This unswerving loyalty between the man at the head of the office and himself was another strong factor in the growth of the Silver Publishing Society.

Of his victory messages, Mr. Banks wrote in *Christ Life*:

"Will you not tell your friends struggling with the

up-and-down life of this wonderful secret given out
of a study of a quarter of a century by the author
and perhaps the last of his larger books, since the Lord
is at the doors. In allowing CHRIST LIFE to publish
these articles serially, Mr. McConkey has done a most
generous thing. The studies are most surely to become
a classic on the subject in hand, as did *The Threefold
Secret of the Holy Spirit*, written in the beginning
of a deeper Christian life. This series on Victory has
taken more of the author's time for meditation and
study than any other book he has ever written. He
says that he believes the sixth, seventh, and eighth
chapters of Romans make up the most profound logic
of any literature, sacred or profane."

Before these studies ever appeared in book form,
there were many heartfelt testimonies as to their effect
on the human heart. A Quakeress from her bed of
suffering told how she had been led to memorize, "Let
not sin therefore reign in your mortal bodies," and
was studying the subject of Victory over sin when the
first of the Victory articles appeared—in the first issue
of *Christ Life* she had seen. She called in a friend to
rejoice with her that the *Lord* had sent her this message in a magazine she had never heard of before. She
immediately subscribed and wrote Mr. McConkey: "I
knew thee had sent it—that wonderful article, *The Way
of Victory*."

In writing of these articles, Mr. Banks said: "These
studies have emerged, as indeed have all of Mr.
McConkey's writings, from the treading of the wine-
press of physical suffering. God has been pleased to
make this author's writings what someone has called
'spiritual classics.' "

When the last of the articles had been published,

Mr. McConkey wrote one of his friends: "I am in real good shape and the work is much easier. Reason—my new book is DONE! And in the hands of the linotype man. So you can imagine what a relief that is. We hope to have it out in the early autumn if the Lord sends the money, which is coming in nicely."

One reason why he and Mr. Banks were congenial spirits was that they were both men of letters and each delighted in the other's gift. When they first met, in a hotel room in Charlotte, N. C., Mr. Banks remembered looking over Mr. McConkey's shoulder while he pored over a list of Anglo-Saxon words from "A" to "R" which he had dug out of the dictionary and preserved for study. He believed the Anglo-Saxon word was always more effective than the derived or Latinized word. The result of this study in the use of words can be seen throughout his printed messages and was one of the factors in promoting a forceful simplicity of style.

When he was alone with his intimate associates, he would talk freely about his books and they learned how dear to his heart were all his printed testimonies. Anything unusual in the way of testimony touched him to the quick. He said that once a friend of his was in a church abroad and before the service began, he noticed a woman in prayer. She spoke in an audible tone and he overheard these words, "Lord, keep me from making unlawful bread!" The friend recognized at once the reference to the phrase used in *The Sure Shepherd* where the author describes it as the bread of unbelief such as Satan tempts us to eat when he offers us stone.

This inner circle of choice friends included a small proportion of missionaries. They were the most faithful of all to express appreciation. Dr. Dorothy Speer, of the Isabella Thoburn College in Lucknow, India, wrote that she had been reading one of the booklets a day for twenty-eight days of her vacation and found it "a mine of spirituality." After asking permission to make translations, she closed by saying how much she would like to send a large gift, but instead could contribute only a dollar bill that had been sent to her from home "to buy candy or something of the sort" on her vacation.

He was impressively grateful for any service, large or small, to himself, but when anything was done for the *work*, his gratitude was multiplied tenfold. After Mr. Buchanan, who was then General Secretary of the Y.M.C.A., in Richmond, had offered the Braille Library a home in his building, Mr. McConkey wrote:

"My warmest Christian love to Mr. Buchanan. Tell him how much I appreciate his lovely kindness in giving us desk room at the 'Y' and that there is no place in the city I would sooner have our work centered than with him. . . . I will surely pray about the interruption to your office work. The Lord will adjust it. The same Lord who gave us the room!"

About the same time, Mr. Banks sent the following note:

"Brother James has received this extremely distressing letter from Richmond and wonders if you could not handle it for him as a piece of personal work. You know how tremendously it takes virtue out of him, so to speak—you remember the Lord's expression when the woman touched him—to write a letter answering a need like this. It would be a twofold ministry if you could help her and him by doing this."

XII

BACK TO RICHMOND (IN 1927)

THE Braille Library had soon outgrown its cramped quarters and for this reason was moved, (in 1927) to the Y.M.C.A. Building. Through the kindness of Mr. Buchanan, the general secretary, free office room was given, and as the work began to develop on a larger scale, none rejoiced in its growth more than the founder. When he arrived in Richmond during the latter part of the winter of 1927, he was full of praise to God for His power in creating this growth, and was always ready to express his appreciation to all who had a part in the work.

In order to do this more effectively, he gave a luncheon at the "Y" to which he invited those who had contributed money and given voluntary service in the office. Facts and figures were discussed around the table, his gratitude for the interest of each one was publicly expressed, and the meeting closed with a chain of prayer for the specific needs. In this luncheon group the two who stood out most prominently were Mr. Robert Friend and Mr. Wade McCargo.

It was most interesting, even edifying, to watch him in a crowd to see how he reacted to the remarks of others. As we passed from the hall into the luncheon room that day, one of his devoted admirers exclaimed,

159

"Oh, we have a Round Table, and this is the King!"
Instead of being pleased with this poetic allusion, as
I thought any man would be, he was undoubtedly
pained. Across his face flitted an expression more
akin to annoyance than anything I had seen there before. Actually, here was a man who did not *want* to
be set up above his fellows, did not want to be king,
figuratively, even! That one expression spoke more
eloquently to my own soul of humility than hundreds
of pages he might have written on the subject. During
the conversation around the table one of the ladies
remarked to him casually, "I suppose it feels good
to know you've become so famous." Again the pained
expression as he answered quietly, "I've left all that,
Mrs. ———, with the Lord."

He had no place for organization from the religion-
ist's point of view, and Mr. McConkey never used the
word in referring to any piece of evangelical work.
His only idea was to receive a vision from God of a
particular need and then to wait on Him for the ways
and means of meeting it. The Braille Library did not
need a board of directors, primarily, but it did need
a prayer group. It needed no schemes for money-
raising, nor even for the management of the office work,
but only a continual looking to God for a revelation
of His plans and a dependence on Him for sustenance.
Naturally the men and women who had shown a helpful
interest in the Library, were the ones to whom he
looked for prayer support, but I do not remember ever
hearing him ask anyone even to pray for it. There was
something in his nature that made him shrink from
soliciting *anything*. Perhaps he knew there was no
use to ask for prayer; those who were going to pray

would pray anyway. They knew he regarded prayer as the first of fundamentals in Christian exercise, so it was not necessary to remind them. So the testimonies of the Lord's goodness through the Braille Library, and the prayers offered around the table resembled a board meeting more than anything the work has ever had.

There were a few in the group who were not familiar with his books, although they were interested in seeing good books made available to the blind. These friends did not realize how well-known Mr. McConkey was throughout Christendom. Certainly there was nothing in his manner to indicate that he enjoyed any higher station than the least of them. Then there were others to whom he represented precisely what God could do with a yielded life. When their praise became too fulsome, he had a way of gently diverting it from himself to the One who deserved it, of teaching the one in error that he himself was no object of praise. On the other hand, he was as much opposed to the criticism of others as he was to the praise of himself. At the same luncheon one of the servants was guilty of an oversight and became the subject of a facetious remark that the Bible had spoken of "the careless Ethiopian." Once more there was the pained expression in the eyes, too fleeting to be noticed by the offender, but inevitable because it must be the register of every hurt in the heart.

But there was one thing that hurt him even more than an injustice to fellow-man and that was any lack of reverence toward God Almighty. At that time we had a public telephone in the Library and an unknown woman stepped in to ask permission to use it. We naturally stopped our conversation as she proceeded with hers, so there was no way to avoid hearing what she said. In the course of the conversation she used some profanity, adding each time, "Excuse my French!" This time the pained expression came and lingered!

In Richmond, as in every other place, his friends were chosen from all classes, and if he was ever conscious of any class distinctions, no one could observe it. There are times when even spiritually-minded men seem unable to avoid a patronizing attitude, but James McConkey always put the most diffident person at ease in his presence. The under-privileged never dreamed that he was inconvenienced by trying to get their viewpoint. They felt that he was one of them. No Southerner ever knew better how to deal with the Negro, to obtain favor among servants. "Uncle Joe," the hoary-headed colored man who for years had been the elevator man at the "Y" often remarked to me, "Yes, Mistis, Mr. McConkey sutny been a good fren' to me." And Mr. McConkey's opinion of him was expressed thus, "I believe Uncle Joe is a real child of the Lord." I shall never forget the look of satisfying pride on Uncle Joe's face each year when Mr. McConkey arrived. He always escorted him from the elevator to the office door, chiefly, I think, to watch the expression of joy that he knew would appear on my face, and to emphasize the fact that he had part in it all. Had he not brought Mr. McConkey up on the elevator?

Mary, the maid who took care of his room, enjoyed doing things for him because he appreciated every little service so much. In speaking of him later, she said, "The principal thing I remember about Mr. McConkey is that he was a mighty good man. Sometimes when he heard me tell the other girls I was hungry, he would give me some money and tell me to go out and get a sandwich. He was the nicest thing in his room. It never was much trouble to clean it up. Every time he came he would give me some of his little books. You could tell he was always thinking about the Lord." Charles, one of the janitors, said, "I've got a pair of shoes that Mr. McConkey gave me the last time he was here. I can't think about him without thinking of the Bible. Seems like he was always talking about the Bible."

It never seemed to occur to him that he was anything but commonplace. Those who knew him intimately persisted in trying to set him on a pedestal, but those who knew him only by sight regarded him as they would any other man, and he took it as a matter of course. He had no eccentricities. His life was normal except for conditions forced upon him by ill health. As we look back now and recall how he fitted himself naturally into the situations about him, into the lives of friends of high and low degrees, we can see how God took this willingness of his to be accounted commonplace for Christ's sake, and used it to make him unique! It was the wedge by which he gained admission into the hearts so that he might make known to them the mysteries of the Gospel. It was the factor by which the messenger was obscured but the message powerfully intensified. If there had been any suggestion of the celebrity about him, the general run of men around the Young Men's Christian Association would have ignored him. But there was none. All they saw was an exceedingly kind man, interested in them personally, and, strange to say, seemed to know Jesus Christ as one man knows another!

This unassumed humility of his was perhaps the factor that contributed most to his popularity with the members of the Richmond "Y". He never asked favors for himself, but Mr. Coles, the desk secretary, found that he enjoyed a certain room on the sixth floor because it was sunny, so he made a point of saving it for him each year. Mr. Wade McCargo (a friend outside) found that he appreciated being driven to his speaking appointments and forthwith appointed himself as Mr. McConkey's chauffeur. Mr. Cook, the chief engineer in the building at that time, in speaking of his spirit, said, "The first time I ever saw Mr. McConkey, I knew he was a Christian man and later I began to suspect that he was the author of some little tracts I had been reading. So I met him one day in the lobby and asked him. When he replied in the affirmative I interrogated him further and said, 'Shall I call you Reverend or Doctor?' 'Just plain Mr. McConkey,' he answered, 'but if you are a Christian, Brother McConkey!' "

If adoring friendship could have spoiled him, he would have been ruined by Howard Banks. Mr. Banks would write his office chief a letter every day to keep him in touch with the Silver Publishing Society. Every line seemed to breathe forth gratitude to the man who had taught him so much about the Lord. But none of these things moved Mr. McConkey! The compliments were ignored in a kindly way, and in speaking of Mr. Banks, he often said, "For years we have been like David and Jonathan and he always insists on making me David."

Mr. Banks was almost as interested as the chief in developing the work among the blind. He suggested our sending a copy of *Chastening* or one of the other books to Helen Keller and asking if we might serve her with the free loan of our books. If she liked them, there was no telling how many other readers she might influence to accept them. How eagerly we watched the mails to receive her reply! Surely her heart would hang on every syllable, and her word was law in the world of the sightless. Seeing people, too, who knew nothing else about the blind always knew something about Helen Keller. They also would look with favor on our work and friends would be raised up among them. Miss Keller had been the means of bringing in thousands of dollars to certain social-service organizations for the blind, so she *might* be used in that same way for this Christian-service organization. We did not know anything about her church affiliation but surely one to whom the whole country paid homage must be a Christian and the type of Christian to appreciate the McConkey books. If she were not already familiar with them, she would surely be eager for more after she had read the first one. Thus she would be our best publicity agent. We had written her that we felt sure such books as these would bring about a spiritual revolution in the world of the blind. We thought she could not help but agree, and agreeing, would act! Thus reasoned the novice-secretary!

The reply came in a polite note from her secretary, thanking us for the book but saying that Miss Keller did not care to receive any more! Later, we found that Miss Keller was a Swedenborgian and still later we had the enlightening experience of reading her

book entitled, *My Religion,* which is a very correct
exposition of Swedenborgianism. In this book, which
has been put into Braille and doubtless has left its
impression on the minds of thousands of blind readers,
she makes clear her opposition to the doctrines of the
substitutionary atonement, to the inspiration of the
Scripture, and to practically all the other essential
elements of the Christian faith. It was easy to understand her lack of enthusiasm for our books.

About dusk one afternoon a very courteous man
called and asked where he might find "Dr. McConkey."
The secretary did not see the exact shade of his complexion so she took him to be a city pastor. Later it
developed that he was "colored"—a professor at Union
University, the Negro college in the suburbs of Richmond. He had come to ask Mr. McConkey to address
the student body there. As usual, the chief took the
secretary into confidence and we discussed together
the possible criticism that might follow especially since
there were so many calls to the whites which must be
turned down. But he was confident that the Lord wanted
him to accept this invitation; so he did.

Besides the callers who came to ask for his services
as speaker, there were many who came merely to express their gratitude to the author of books and tracts
that had been the means of producing a vital change
in their lives. One woman brought her two little boys,
and he listened with keen interest as they were called
upon to recite Bible verses for him. The Word, to
him, was always spirit and life whether it came in
the quiet hours of reading and meditation or from
the faltering lips of a child. There was something in
his manner that reassured the most timid and invited

them to open their hearts to him. One young lady, after telling how she had been led to yield her life by the reading of his books, said, "None of them helped me any more than *Chastening.* I think I must be the kind of child that requires a lot of 'child-training,' Mr. McConkey." "I'm just that kind of fellow, myself, Miss H.," he answered.

So, with delivering oral messages, seeing callers, directing the Braille Library, and keeping oversight of the Silver Publishing Society, there was not a great deal of time left for writing and undoubtedly the printed messages were the most important part of the work because they were to be his legacy to the world. Each one must, first of all, be a faithfully recorded *message,* no concoction of man's brain. Then it must be plain, "so simple," he said, "that it can be understood by the most ignorant colored preacher"; yet each one must have a literary finish that would satisfy the most fastidious critic. He maintained a high literary standard through the years and had no intention of lapsing now. Beside all this, there was his "sawdust head," as he called it, to be reckoned with—still no more than thirty minutes a day of work on the written messages. Otherwise, one of the dreaded headaches would be sure to return with several days of inactivity. This was what the public was slow to understand. When people saw him walking around in the line of duty, they concluded there was no reason why his date-book should not be filled. Little did they realize how carefully he must husband his limited strength in order to make it count mightily for the glory of God. How careful he must be not to bring on a breakdown which might mean even years of inactivity! All they knew was that blessing always attended his meetings, and they wanted their share.

One day the office door swung open and Mr. B——, a man we knew very slightly, burst in with, "I want to ask your advice about something. I hardly ever ask anybody's advice and when I do I don't take it. But listen, what do you think of my putting Mr. McConkey's picture in the paper, along with the announcement of his address Friday night?"

Of course the advice he wanted was an approval of his plan, but I simply told him that I had heard Mr. McConkey say he did not care to have his picture in the newspapers and for that reason had never allowed a cut to be made. I felt quite sure he would much prefer the simple announcement, unaccompanied by a photograph. Strange to say, Mr. B—— took the hint.

Richmond people with typical southern courtesy paid him the highest compliment of which they were capable. They welcomed him into their circles as one of them! Even the old Irreconcilables forgot he was a Northerner when once they had felt the warmth of his smile. One day a lady who was one of his most enthusiastic admirers was speaking of the author and his books to a rabid old Southerner, when he chanced to inquire about Mr. McConkey's native soil. Upon hearing that he was a Pennsylvanian, the old gentleman shrugged his shoulders and said, "Ugh, a Yankee, is he!" But this was the only case on record where any Richmonder ever considered him as other than "one of us." No doubt if this man had exchanged a few words with him, he too would have forgotten the significance of "The Line." Mr. McConkey loved the South and was only amused by little differences in non-essentials such as certain pronunciations and expressions.

Neither the friends in his offices nor those who knew him less intimately ever had the feeling that he was exerting himself to come down to their level. They only knew they felt at ease with him as did other untaught Christians among whom was a colored porter from a hotel near the "Y". This man came over frequently for little chats with Mr. McConkey and always carried away a package of tracts for distribution. Just after the porter had left, one day, he said to me, "I'm glad my books are acceptable to him, it's a good test for them."

Occasionally, children came to the office of the Library. He always treated them not as inferiors or superiors but rather as equals. Edna Durrette, a twelve-year-old girl, had been helping with the wrapping so he thanked her for this, asked her about her Sunday school and gave her an autographed copy of one of the simpler tracts. As she walked home that evening, Edna had no idea that she had talked with a great man—she only knew he was kind. In speaking of his love for children, he said, "Whenever I tell Blanche (his sister, Mrs. C. M. Kerr) I have a new sweetheart, she says right away, 'Yes, I suppose she's about ten years old!' "

It was not his contacts with children that took so much out of him but those with older people who would ask favors of him without realizing the wear and tear this meant to his nervous system. When he promised to pray about a matter, it did not mean that he would mention it casually to God once or twice; it meant that he was going to pray through with you! Few realized this when they asked for his prayer-help. As he rarely mentioned his physical weakness, thoughtless friends would call on him to make visits which consumed a great deal more nervous energy than he had to spare. One young woman concerned about the spiritual indifference of her fiance, urged Mr. McConkey to visit him in the hope that the young man might catch something of the influence of this winsome teacher. Mr. McConkey considered it a rather useless mission, as it proved to be, but because she asked it, he went. The man was only a nominal Christian and had no time for anything vital—hardly time to be polite. The young woman realized afterwards that she should not have taxed Mr. McConkey's strength in this way. She appreciated so much his never reproving her for it that ever afterward she avoided asking him, or any other Christian worker, to do anything. His quiet acquiescence was the very thing for her as well as for him.

He always had means to meet his necessary expenses though it was a known fact that he would allow no solicitation for himself or his work. Some people were amazed at this, marveled at the way God took care of a man who never asked for anything, losing sight of the fact that possibly God might use them to supply his need. If they had received spiritual blessing, it might be their responsibility to minister with their possessions. So it was that several groups called on him to speak for them without ever giving him an offering of any kind. They knew he depended on the Lord to take care of him, so why should they bother? They were quite right. The Lord did take care of him, supplying every need whether the group receiving the benefit of his labor was willing to be used in it or not. When groups failed, individuals were used. On one occasion, just after a succession of meetings, in which an offering seemed to have been far from the minds of the congregation, one of his devoted friends from another church called him aside and gave him a generous amount—which was most gratefully received. Any offering made voluntarily touched him deeply but when a gift came like this, from one of his spiritual sons, the atmosphere was simply charged with his appreciation. It helped heal the hurt which must have been in his heart because of the indifference of others. Whenever an offering came, the conviction was deepened that this was the Lord's way for him to live. It, undoubtedly, was not His way for many other of His children, but it was for *him*. One reason was that it kept him dependent upon God, The First Cause. Another was that it kept him closely linked with his fellow-men. He was conscious of a definite obligation to those who were prompted by the Spirit to give generously of their means to him. It worked both ways. Friends who had been helped by his ministry gave him money and he gave back to them love and appreciation. In this way, a friendship was established on the foundation of mutual service. Undoubtedly he would have had fewer warm, personal, loving friends if his support had come in an impersonal way from some organization. As it was, he entered unobtrusively into their hearts, always making them feel that he was the debtor, so that even those who knew him casually could not speak of him without saying "*Dear*" Mr. McConkey."

God was not only the first cause in financial matters but in all others. This was impressed on the mind of a young woman who met him on the bus one day and wanted very much to talk with him but had not known how to get in touch with him. She had been brought to the place of surrender by means of his books and his public addresses but she was a nurse and had little time for private interviews, although she longed to know him better and to learn more of the Lord from his lips. When they parted that afternoon, she said, "I'm so glad I happened to run into you, Mr. McConkey."

"It was the Lord, Miss Bessie," he replied. That settled it.

Another of his spiritual children said to him something like this: "Mr. McConkey, if certain types of Christians that I know had tried to lead me to the Lord, I'd never in this world have followed. The Lord knew it would take a personality like yours—a combination of forcefulness and winsomeness, for me. No other instrument would have been effective."

He smiled slowly with that expression of inner joy that must have been his whenever he thought of another trophy won, and said, "Well, I don't know of anything that will give me greater joy, Miss H., than to present you to the Lord Jesus."

XIII

LAST YEARS IN RICHMOND

How FULL those winters of 1928 and 1929 were
for him! But no matter how many speaking engagements and private interviews there were, he never failed
to come to the Library once a day. The work was still
too new for me to serve as a full-time worker. I spent
only the latter part of each afternoon there. Small as
it was, however, he recognized in it the germ of greatness and did not despise it. He saw groping fingers
in all parts of the world, searching out the truth on
those embossed pages and darkened lives brightening
up a bit because of that truth. How eagerly I looked
forward to his coming each afternoon when about five
o'clock, the door would open gently and there he would
stand in his overcoat, hat in hand. After he had deposited the hat and overcoat on a chair, he would seat
himself awkwardly on another. He had big feet, even
for his big body, and always wore ugly, high-topped
shoes which stood out above everything else he wore.
Apart from this, there was nothing particularly noticeable about his appearance—just a well-groomed, gray-
haired, gray-mustached, gentle-voiced man. In repose,
his face gave no token of the deep wells of joy be-
neath. He said to me once, "You know books always
have their watermark. Well, the watermark of mine

173

is suffering." I thought as he said it that the same suffering was written in his flesh although overruled by the Spirit.

Our conversation usually turned to the oral message the night before (if there had been one), and I told him just what parts of it had found lodgment in my heart and in the hearts of others who had expressed themselves about it. He was keen on reactions. He did not want a message printed unless he knew something about the spiritual response of his hearers. He was no respecter of persons, just so *someone* had been helped, it made no difference how weak a Christian he might be. By this time, my contacts with him were strengthening my own faith and enabling me the better to discern false teaching. I often asked him about other speakers and writers, whether they were Scripturally sound or not. If he knew them, he never failed to express his conviction—they were "true-to-the-Word," or "middle-of-the-road," or "Modernistic." I hung on every syllable, with never a thought of distrusting his judgment. I knew it would be given conservatively, charitably, and only on request. When he saw a man slipping, who hitherto had stood firmly for sound doctrine, it hurt so deeply, he could hardly speak of it, and when he saw Modernistic leaders slipping into positions of trust in Christian organizations, there was too much agony of soul to give room for idle criticism of those who allowed it. To him, Modernism was the most subtle enemy the cause of Christ could have, but he would give Modernists no chance to say, "Modernists may lack clarity, but Fundamentalists lack charity." He would prove to them that a man could stand upon clearly defined doctrinal principles and still be warmly charitable. He would fight them, not with bitter words, but constructive teaching, and this he did fully both in private and public. Those who sat at his feet unconsciously imbibed a distrust of Modernism and a love for God's Word in its entirety.

After we discussed the varied reactions to his messages, he looked over the mail and was as delighted over the "blessing letters" as if they had been something entirely new to him. However, there was something novel about these letters. Although people in almost every other condition of adversity had written about the help they had received from his books, there had never been letters from the blind until the launching of this Library. One day there came an adverse criticism. A blind woman somewhere in the West wrote that she had read *Chastening* and that the illustration the author gave about breaking the sheep's leg was not true to life. She knew all about sheep and this was not natural. The author had botched things in this respect. If such a criticism had come from the highest literary tribunal, he would not have regarded it with more concern. He said he had established his authority before he used the incident and felt sure the critic was mistaken, therefore, he would not change it. Well did James McConkey know what it meant for the Shepherd to break a body for the sake of breaking a will and his face grew graver as he spoke of it, while perhaps the pain in his heart lingered as he went to his room that night with the thought that this time his message had not accomplished its purpose.

Others who wrote letters did not reveal a critical attitude, but merely said, "I don't like these religious books. Please don't send me any more." But for the

most part, the letters were rich with testimony of how
the Lord had used these Braille messages in their lives.
One day a card came from the Reverend Ernest P.
Janvier, Ph.D., a blind missionary to India, saying:
"I understand that some of James H. McConkey's tracts
are now in Braille. If so, may I borrow them? Mr.
McConkey was a dear friend of my father's at
Princeton."

His father was the "Janvier" referred to by Dr.
Frost earlier in these pages, the "Jan" whom Jim
McConkey had known and loved in college days. After
he had received the books, Dr. Janvier wrote:
"Dear Mr. McConkey:

"I feel that I know you, not only as my father's
friend but also through your devotional messages which
have come to me from time to time in Braille from
Richmond, Virginia. These messages I have found
very helpful to my own soul, and I have wanted to
make them available to my Indian brethren. I have
just finished translating *The Fifth Sparrow* into simple
Urdu and the editor of 'The Star of India' has kindly
consented to print it in his Christian (M.E.) periodical.
I hope you have no objection."

One day he brought to the office a letter received fifteen years before from Thomas A. Edison, acknowledg-
ing the receipt of *Give God a Chance,* which has on its
first pages an illustration taken from the life of Mr.
Edison. Mr. McConkey remarked: "The Lord has laid
it upon my heart to write Edison a letter and urge upon
him the acceptance of Christ as his Savior."

A copy of the letter was not kept but in substance
it was something like this:

"I wish to write and thank you for the benefit I

have received from your Ediphone. For years I have been writing devotional messages and on account of being subject to brain-fag, could not write with comfort more than fifteen minutes a day. Now, by means of the Ediphone, I can dictate for half an hour at a time; so my power of production has been doubled by means of your invention." Then he urged upon this idol of the public acceptance in simple faith of the Son of God as his Savior. Mr. Edison was to him, as he wrote, not a mighty man of science causing millions to stand in amazement before his productions, but simply a lost soul for whom Christ had died, and he was dealt with as such, not uncompromisingly nor harshly, but positively and gently. No answer ever came but one thing is sure—Thomas A. Edison who went into eternity without a profession of faith in the Son of God could not stand before the Judge of all the earth and say, "No one ever showed me the way."

It was in private conversations in the office or in the home, rather than in public addresses, that one was able to get his views on many other things besides Modernism. He never ranted against worldliness but one could hardly sit under his messages day after day and continue in questionable amusements. He had very little to say about such things, even in private, unless his opinion was asked, but everyone knew there was no place in his life for them, that every hour in every day was given over to seeking "a city which hath foundations." One afternoon as we sat in the Library, a newsboy rushed in with his papers and Mr. McConkey bought one. So he picked up a pencil and paper from the desk and wrote, "Please give me fifteen cents to go to the movies." Since he was a deaf-mute, the conversation had to be in writing. Knowing Mr. McConkey's tender sympathy for the blind and the deaf and all the physically handicapped, I wondered what he would do, but there was no hesitation on his part. He handed me the pencil and said, "Tell him that as a Christian I cannot support the movies, in any way. The system is too corrupt."

The only other time I ever heard him speak of movies was when he found that several young women in the city who expected to enter definite Christian work had deliberately chosen to go to a picture show rather than to hear a great Christian leader who was lecturing that evening. As he spoke of it, his face showed only pain. There was no thought of criticism, but rather grief that they had so misjudged values!

It is related that a lady friend of his youth met him years afterwards and in the course of the conversation said, "James, are you keeping up with the Thaw murder case?"

"No, Mattie," he answered, "I never read things like that." There was no reproof in the tone, but honesty demanded a statement of facts. He had no time for such things. Moreover, he had warned others about meeting sin at the gateway of the imagination, so he must heed his own warning.

He had said publicly something to the effect that those who fill their minds with the newspaper on Sunday mornings have no room left for the things of God. A reporter came to the office one afternoon and offered to give a full write-up of the Braille Library to appear in the next Sunday's issue, but he was as firm as he was gentle in his refusal. "No," he said, "the people who are likely to become vitally interested in our work don't read Sunday newspapers; we would prefer not to have any publicity than to have it on Sunday." The reporter considered this rank fanaticism and grudgingly gave a very meager account of the work for the blind in one of the week-day issues. He was unusually light-hearted after a decision had been reached or after a special piece of work had been completed. One after-noon, he came in announcing that *The Way of Victory* had been finished at last. "And," he added, "I feel like throwing up my hat and buying a dish of ice-cream to celebrate." The "sawdust head" had been giving a good deal of trouble so it was a tremendous relief to know that the creative part had been done—publishers and office force could now do the mechanical!

He was noticeably sensitive to garrulous people who talked much and said little. He protected his head and nervous system by avoiding such persons. The avoid-ance, however, was managed in such a deferential way that no one could take offense. A typical case will serve as illustration: A certain flighty lady was ready to take possession of him one Sunday morning after he had spoken in one of the churches. She had some theory she wished to discuss which probably would have consumed a great deal of time after the service, and to no purpose whatever except to vent her opinions. He listened for a few minutes and then turned her over to a Christian woman standing near-by with the atti-tude that "Miss N. can tell you about this just as well or better than I can." The talkative woman was not pleased, but his manner was so deferential, she had to accept the situation and say nothing. She had ex-pected to monopolize the speaker of the morning and here he had turned her over to some obscure person

while he was speaking to other people! If she had
been a sincere seeker after truth, however ignorant or
humble, he no doubt would have asked her to make
an appointment with him so they might talk undis-
turbed; but he was not eager to make engagements
for the purpose of hearing nebulous views, so the lady
floated out of his life as airily as she had floated in.

At the same church, a young woman whose whole
life had been transformed by reading *The Surrendered
Life*, sat in the choir and hung eagerly on every
word. After the benediction, she went down quickly
to shake hands and thank him for the message. His
face lighted up as it always did when he knew his
words had "gone home," but immediately his attention was upon her as he said, "Yes, and I got a blessing
from that beautiful song, too, Miss Margaret."

During those later years when the richness of his
experience was felt so strongly by all who knew him,
one might have expected large and promising audiences
for him; but not so. His audiences, for the most part,
were not striking in any respect. Yet scattered among the
conventional church-going group were friends who had
caught the gleam from the lamp of truth he had been
holding before them. Such eagerly sought more light.
Although the numbers were seldom large, the proportion of earnest seekers for truth was considerable.
This was what he wished. He knew the masses were
not eager for a message which fitted only the inner
circle. Really, he seemed not to care whether the
church were fashionable or plain, the crowd large or
small, the introduction a fitting one or not, but he did
care tremendously about the response. He was happy
to have people speak to him at the close of the service

and ask about Scripture passages they wished to have clarified, to tell him how they had already been straightened out on certain points, and how certain parts of the message had gripped their hearts.

Of course, Mr. McConkey did not win all his hearers, but even those who opposed his message were disarmed by his courtesy and charity. Outspoken Modernists had nothing to say against the man himself and usually refrained from the patronizing attitude adopted as a last resort. The Sunday morning when he gave *God-Given Men* in one of the large Presbyterian churches, there was in the congregation a theological student with decidedly Modernistic tendencies who had come at the invitation of a young woman who was one of Mr. McConkey's devotees. With a good deal of curiosity, this student began to study the personality of the man in the pulpit—his scholarship, culture, determination, but above all, his charity in every line! As usual, he had not appeared that morning until the preliminaries were almost over, and though never a word was said about it, one knew instinctively this twenty or thirty minutes had been spent in intensive prayer. As he went on with this message on soul-winning, pouring into it all the earnestness of which he was capable, the young man must have missed the eulogy on the natural man and the emphasis on the social gospel which he had been accustomed to hear from his own leaders. It seemed strange to see this older man with his decided gifts speaking as if there were only one important service in a Christian's life around which everything else revolved and that was just the old-fashioned business of bringing men to Jesus Christ. Their paths did not cross again and there has been no

evidence of change in the younger man. The same,
no doubt, might be said of others who heard him once.

The only "parlor-meeting" of Mr. McConkey's that
I ever attended was one held under the auspices of
a woman's auxiliary of St. James Episcopal Church.
He might have appeared embarrassed — a solitary
bachelor among thirty or thirty-five women—if he had
not, as usual, been bent upon his task. He did seem
a little awkward in the beginning, but this was soon
overlooked as the listeners were more and more en-
raptured with the thought of resurrection victory. Perhaps they caught something of the ecstasy that was his
when he quoted: "So when this corruptible shall have
put on incorruption and this mortal shall have put on
immortality, then shall be brought to pass the saying
that is written, Death is swallowed up in victory"—
and as he went on to the climax: "The dead in Christ
shall rise first. Then we which are alive and remain
shall be caught up *together with them*!" When he
quoted those last three words, his eyes closed and we
fancied that already, in imagination, he was joining
his precious mother and other loved ones who had gone
ahead and was standing even then on the threshold of
the presence of the Lord Himself! There was a holy
hush over the room as there always was at the close
of his meetings. The atmosphere was not conducive
to small talk—only to the expression of gratitude for
spiritual light received. When she told him good-by,
the hostess of the "parlor-meeting" slipped ten dollars into his hand to show the interest of her group in
the work of the Braille Library. When we talked it
over the next day, I demurred about accepting the
money for the Library. (The woman's statement had

been somewhat ambiguous and no doubt she would have been glad to have him use it for personal needs but did not know just how to tell him so.) He laid the money on the desk and said with a trace of humor, "No, I can't divert the use of funds!"

In those days, the Library was having very little publicity: word concerning it was passed on in much the same way the Gospel story was given by individuals in the first century. Mr. McConkey would tell certain friends about it as he had done at the parlor-meeting and almost invariably, those friends would respond by action of some kind. One of these was Mr. R. H. Purnell, who became interested after he had heard a little about the work and went to the "Y" for more information. Mr. McConkey took him into the office to show him some of the Braille books and to give more details about the plan of work. When he stopped talking, Mr. Purnell said, "I feel as if I ought to do something about this but I am not sure what it is."

"Suppose we kneel here and ask the Lord to guide you into whatever His will is about it," replied Mr. McConkey.

When they got up from their knees, the visitor said, "I want to have *Give God a Chance* put into Braille. You said the cost of forty copies would be around twenty-eight dollars, so I'll send you my check for that amount."

That was the way the money came, though seldom in such large amounts. If ever a person was "sold" to anything, Mr. McConkey was sold to the voluntary offering plan. The thought of anyone's soliciting for the Lord's work was repugnant to his mind. To go out and beg for work carried on in the name of Christ was to him just another "work of the flesh," a thing dishonoring to the Lord. When he talked with friends about the Silver Publishing Society and the Braille Library, it was only with reference to the service rendered from these offices, never a hint of any sort about money. We were discussing this in the office one day and his face showed real distress as he thought of how some Christians bungled things by constant reliance on the arm of flesh. He said, "You know Hudson Taylor used to say, 'Be God's man, in God's place, doing God's work, in God's way'—and that means 'God's woman' too, you know. It's amazing how some of God's men who are doing God's work simply will not do it God's way, and the result is He is not glorified."

In the winter of 1929, Mrs. Mortimer Lane made a three or four days visit to Richmond, meanwhile making an intensive personal campaign with the tracts. Elevator operators, bell-boys, street-car motormen, and people she met in a social way were thus introduced to the McConkey publications. Mr. Lane was Secretary of the Silver Publishing Society at that time and his letters about affairs in the office were a pure delight to his Chief. Mrs. Lane had several speaking appointments while she was in Richmond and as he sat in the audience, Mr. McConkey had the joy of hearing her tell back some of the great spiritual truths he had told her. Once after she had spoken in another city, a friend remarked, "If I hadn't seen the speaker, I would certainly have thought it was James McConkey giving the message."

Like the rest of his spiritual children, the Lanes were peculiarly dear to him. He had led them into the light and their gratitude to him as God's instrument, was unbounded. To love him was to love the Silver Publishing Society. You could hardly separate the two. After Mrs. Lane had gone back to Pittsburgh, she wrote him a jubilant note about the amount of the weekly offering. As he laid the letter aside and took off his glasses, he said, "Yes, and I suspect she put in the extra herself."

His last few weeks in Richmond, after Mrs. Lane's return to Pittsburgh, were perhaps the busiest of the whole year. All sorts of requests for advice and service came to him, one of which was an invitation to speak to a group which he considered radical, not in the sense that they were Modernistic, but, we might say, radical in their profession of personal holiness and in their emotional reaction to religion. He did not accept the invitation, and a few days later a man who was earnestly seeking the truth came to him and asked him what he thought of the group whose invitation he had not accepted. "Well," he replied gravely, "they have some real Christians among them, undoubtedly, but I have never yet found one who could explain the experience which they say sets them apart from other yielded Christians. Their doctrine of eradication is not held by the best Bible teachers and I, personally, do not believe it is Scriptural. So I thought it was best for me not to go to them with my message."

This frank statement would never have been made had it not been solicited, for he did not raise his voice against any sect unless it became necessary. If they preached salvation through the blood, he could still call them brethren although he could not approve the un-Scriptural elements in their doctrine, nor subscribe

to some of their practices. In the light of these facts
he did not deem it wise to speak in their churches.
Since his strength was so limited, it was surely the
will of God for him to place his efforts where they
would count for most.

Nor did he mention slight doctrinal differences between himself and other theologians of the same school
unless he was pressed for a statement. One friend,
after reading one of Dr. Campbell Morgan's books in
which the belief of a "partial rapture" was set forth,
sat down immediately and wrote Mr. McConkey for
his views on the matter. In his reply, he minimized
the differences between Dr. Morgan and himself and
stated in a few words that he had never been able to
see that the Scripture made any distinction in this
regard between babes in Christ and the most spiritual
Christians.

It was surprising how the "babes" drank in his deeper
teaching sometimes. One little girl nine years old heard
one of his messages on consecration in which he said,
"The best illustration of consecration that I know is
to write your name on a blank piece of paper and then
leave it for the Lord to fill in, to let Him send into your
life whatever He will." The next day when her mother
was telling her about the blank paper, she opened her
eyes wide and said, "I've done it!"

This same mother told him that she had decided
to turn over to the Silver Publishing Society a diamond
bracelet which had been given her by her husband.
Since she had found Christ sufficient, and this chiefly
by means of his teaching, the ephemeral charms of a
glamorous society had faded for her and she really
had very little use for any kind of jewelry in her

new life. The bracelet was valued at three thousand dollars.

He had no set program during that last winter. In fact, he never made the slightest effort to get a speaking appointment but waited until he was sought, then laid each invitation before God, learned His mind about each and gave his answer. It was impossible for him to keep pace with some of his physically-strong friends who could speak three or four times a day without exhaustion, and he frankly told them so. When Mr. Walter Fraser, of Pittsburgh, stopped over in Richmond for a day or two, Mr. McConkey took him out to the Union Theological Seminary to make an address, and he said in speaking of their visit together, "I told Walter he need not expect me to keep up with him—a forty-horse power, and I, about a half-horse!"

Not one person in a hundred realized what the interviews took out of him. They could understand his refusal to accept speaking appointments but an interview seemed to them to be such a little thing, so he did his best to meet the demand. Often the problems were purely personal, but he always used them as a basis for teaching some spiritual truth. Miss G. wrote him of a difference that had come between herself and her *fiance* and asked him to pray about it, little realizing how many other people had done the same thing; but he wrote back: "I note your request for prayer, Miss G., and will gladly take care of it. Meanwhile, if you feel like acquainting me more fully with the circumstances of the case, I shall be glad to do anything I can in the way of personal counsel. However, that is entirely with you."

Later on, after he had talked with her, he wrote:

"I have been praying about your problems. The Father will solve them for you, lassie. He never fails us, even though He keeps us waiting. My dear child, just you trust God in that personal matter so close to your heart. He will never fail a child of His so dear to Him as you are. The Lord bless you and give you His very best; you who are 'accepted in the Beloved.'"

Fortunately, not all his letters were from those who made demands upon him. During these days he received more and more testimonies to the value of his printed messages as well as many personal assurances of intercessory prayer, and there was nothing on earth that he valued quite as much. Some of those who wrote knew about the battle he was constantly waging for health and assured him of their remembrance of this at the Throne. But all wrote of how they were praying for the messages to be circulated more widely and to find lodgment in more hearts. As he listened to the reading of one of these from a woman some distance away, his face revealed gratitude and humility until he heard a sentence which savored of the glorification of man, then there were the marks of serious displeasure. The letter was spoiled for him the moment there was a suspicion that any glory was given to James McConkey and not to his Lord.

There was no danger of anything of that kind in the letters of Miss Louisa Graham, of England! While each one was overflowing with joy and gratitude because she had discovered such rich deposits of truth in his books, there was never a failure to recognize the fact that the author was only a tool used by the Divine. His strength would not permit him to answer the letters, but each one received a reply from his office either in Pittsburgh or in Richmond, assuring her of his gratitude for her prayers. Miss Graham was an invalid who had not walked for years and one of her letters telling of her "joy-rides" in the invalid's chair while she gave out tracts in the park, was published in leaflet form by the Silver Publishing Society. The whole leaflet is permeated with the influence of *Chastening* upon her life, and it is easy to see that his words about "child-training" had entered her soul and helped her to realize the "peaceable fruit" borne by those who accept chastening as such.

XIV

LAST YEARS

AFTER Mr. Banks had given up his work as Secretary of the Silver Publishing Society in order to take over the publishing of *Christ Life* Magazine, Mr. Mortimer B. Lane took his place (in January, 1929). The office work was heavy enough to warrant the employment of three young ladies, and often Mrs. Lane, as a voluntary helper. What a satisfaction it was to Mr. McConkey to see the work moving forward so rapidly! But in the midst of it all he became conscious of a physical slipping. Perhaps he had filled too many engagements in Richmond; at any rate there had been too much strain. It was telling on him. The old headaches were coming back in intensified and lengthening form. He was forced to drop all speaking and much writing. He took a longer summer vacation than usual; but nothing seemed to help. There was just a gradual ebbing of strength.

He continued to live in the East Liberty "Y" until the summer, when he and his sister, Mrs. Charles Kerr, went to Eaglesmere for a prolonged vacation. While there, he did not seem to improve as they had hoped. In fact, his bodily strength was so impaired that Mrs. Kerr sent an urgent call to her husband to come to Eaglesmere and assist in taking him home to Wrightsville. The trip, made in easy stages, required two or three days but at last he was safe in his sister's home. Those were long, weary days which followed for he sensed that it was the beginning of the end. Mrs. Kerr herself was not well and her sister-in-law, Miss Sallie Kerr, served six weeks as nurse for her and Mr. McConkey. There were times when the nervousness was so intense that his nights were practically sleepless. He asked permission of his devoted friends, Misses Sallie and Ella Kerr, to stay in their home at night as it was on a more quiet street than that of his sister. This plan was abandoned, however, and he continued for some weeks with his "dear sister," as he always called Mrs. Kerr. However, the large old-fashioned home of the Misses Kerr on Third Street was always a favorite retreat with him. It was here that the McConkeys and Kerrs had played together as children, and two of the sons of the house of Kerr had married daughters of the house of McConkey, so the families were very close. These friends were like sisters to him for they had watched his career with joy and satisfaction and had prayed continuously for his work. Now all prayer was directed toward his restoration to health.

There was little improvement, if any, and the question uppermost in Mr. McConkey's mind was whether he should return to Pittsburgh or remain in Wrightsville. Finally, after much prayer, and, knowing that the journey could be made in easy stages, he decided to go. Shortly after his return to Pittsburgh he faced another momentous decision. The effectual and fervent prayers of his friends for guidance helped him in these days of crises. It seemed clear to him that the wise plan was to go to Hillsview Sanitarium at Washington, Pennsylvania, thirty miles from Pittsburgh.

Here, his devoted sister saw that every attention was lavished upon him, and she herself wrote to him every day from her home in Wrightsville. This brother and sister were the only surviving members of a family of thirteen children, and the two were peculiarly dear to each other. She never neglected any need of his, and in addition never forgot little luxuries, such as flowers on his birthday and chocolates at frequent intervals. She was always his "little sister" and his letters to her began, "Dear Blanchie" or "Dear Sweetheart."

After he had been at Hillsview some months, Mr. and Mrs. Kerr received a telegram which took them immediately to him. They found him unconscious. Mr. Kerr went into the room with an unconcerned manner in order not to alarm him. He was not alarmed, but much surprised as he asked, "Why, Charley, what are you doing here?"

"Oh, just passing through and stopped over to see you," Mr. Kerr replied.

That satisfied him but, as usual, his next thought was for his sister so he asked, "Where's Blanchie?" and went on with the conversation. The day before, Mrs. Kerr had despaired of his life but now in answer to prayer, he had "come back." This rally of his again gave encouragement to those who loved him, but there was never anything like a return to normal strength.

It is not necessary to go into the details of his suffering. Only those who have undergone such a breakdown know what it means—sleepless nights, pain, and depression! But after two years of rest and rebuilding of tissues, there came some improvement. Friends around the world were praying and it seemed for awhile as if the Lord were beginning to raise him up. But in the summer of 1932, he fell and broke his hip. More weeks of intense suffering followed during which it seemed impracticable to put the hip in a cast, so his period of helplessness was necessarily lengthened. As he lay on his bed for months, helpless and often in agony, praying friends became encouraged by the mere fact that he had passed through the first stages and the bones had begun to knit. In the hope that the Lord would raise him up, a room was reserved for him at Bethany House, a Bible-teaching center and the home of the Silver Publishing Society staff.

In the meantime, Mr. Lane had found it necessary to give up his work in the office and take his family to Southern France for the winter. He was succeeded by Mr. Frank S. Gardner, a business man and friend of many years, who made frequent visits to the Sanitarium and kept Mr. McConkey in touch with the affairs of the office, constantly reminding him of the volume of prayer being sent up for him from all parts of the world.

By the fall of 1933, he was able to move about in a rolling chair and to take a few steps. With some measure of release from pain, the depression was lifted and he began again to rejoice in the Word. Mr. Gardner would bring to him for consideration, all matters of importance connected with the Pittsburgh office and the Secretary of the Braille Library kept him in close touch with the Richmond office by correspondence. After giving his attention to these matters, there was very little strength left for anything else, but he managed to get in a little writing now and then—usually

a short editorial for *Christ Life*. The only full-sized
pamphlet written during his illness was his *Notes on
Ephesians,* given to him in answer to many hundreds
of praying friends around the world.

They were lonely days at Hillsview Farms except
when friends from Pittsburgh drove out to see him.
Mr. Banks had gone Home ahead of him, something
neither of them had anticipated, but there were many
other friends in Pittsburgh, the very sight of whom
would brighten the whole day for him. These visits,
his letter-writing, his reading, Bible-study, and prayer
filled up the days. In his letters, he had very little
to say about himself—usually some statement like this
at the end, "My condition is about the same," but he
was ready to give any counsel requested in regard to the
work of the Library. He was not informed, of course,
of the details of the extreme financial pressure from
1932 to 1935, but he saw the figures on the report
and marveled at the way the Lord had caused it to
expand when so little cash was available. The same
was true of the Silver Publishing Society. Then, as
always, his first thought was of the office force—
whether or not their salaries were sufficient. When he
grew a little apprehensive about this, he wrote . . .
"But the God of Hudson Taylor will surely provide
for you!"

On Easter Sunday, 1937, a group of friends from
Bethany House went out to Washington to visit him
and took him an Easter lily. When they were all
assembled in the room, he noticed that one young
woman was standing. He was much concerned about
this apparent oversight until he learned that she had
come to sing to him. After the song, they read to him

from the Book he knew so well and together they talked about the things of Christ.

These friends were still hoping beyond hope that before another Easter, he would be safely housed in Bethany but he seemed to have a presentiment that it would never be. Several times during that spring and summer he wrote in the midst of great weakness that he felt sure the Lord's time for his leaving this earth had come. Then he would rally again and write to say that perhaps he would be spared awhile longer, but he was always quite certain that the end was not very far distant and his activity was over. As he had seen so clearly God's plan for his life in years of service, so now he saw the plan at the end far more distinctly than we who hoped that the days of his flesh might be prolonged. As we look back upon it, we see little in these years for the outward man except loneliness, suffering, deprivation and painful detachment from the work he loved better than life itself. Just before he was released from it all, his old friend, Mr. William H. Ridgway, of Coatesville, Pennsylvania, who had lost touch with him for a good many years, wrote him the following letter which, however, was never read with his eyes of clay:

"Sept. 20, 1937

"My dear Jim:

. . . . "I am just dropping you a line to slap you on the shoulder, as it were, and say, 'Hello, old-timer, here's to you.'

"Say, Jim, a whole lot of water has gone down the Susquehanna River since the day you came to Coatesville, a part of a little local Y.M.C.A. conference, and put up with Bob Haines, and turned up in my Bible class. That was the beginning of both of us in a sort of public way.

"You became the eye-opener of Bible conferences of the Association of Shickelimmy, on the bluff above Sunbury, at Bloomsburg, Eaglesmere, and other points, where you had the early morning service. Then you put your talks into print and became famous.

"I have kept on in the Y.M.C.A. work and have been writing the Sunday-school lessons for the *Sunday School Times* for some thirty years and am now over eighty-one years of age and still going strong. However, I never know when the Lord will say to me, 'Well done, good and faithful servant. I am going to lay you aside for a little while, like your old friend, Jim McConkey.'

"I have written a book of which I know you will not approve because one of the last addresses I heard you make at one of the Bible conferences, where a lot of us were joking and having some fun, was on that text somewhere there in Corinthians—my concordance is not here at the office—where it talks about foolish jesting.

"The title is *The Christian Gentleman*. Before I was a Christian, some people who were very much interested in me would give me religious books like yours, for example, *The Threefold Secret of the Holy Spirit*, or some other. In order to save my face, I would read the first chapter and then my auntie would say, 'How do you like the book?' I would say, 'Auntie, I haven't finished it yet.' And then afterward I would dodge her and I never would read any more of the book. Why should I, an unregenerate man, be interested in anything religious? Just as the Book says, 'They are all foolishness to him who perisheth.'

"Remembering this, I have undertaken to write a religious book which would be fundamental and evangelical and one which the hard-boiled, rough-neck, irreligious fellow, in college and out of it, in mill or on the race track, will read. Whether I have succeeded or not, results will tell.

"Now even though I feel sure you cannot approve of the book any more than you could approve of my behavior sometimes, especially my tobacco habit (I have not used tobacco for years) yet I would like to send you a copy of the first edition if I am sure of your address. All you have to do is to dictate to your nurse, in case you cannot write yourself, and say something like this, 'Dear Bill: Send along *The Christian Gentleman*. If I could stand you in the years gone by, in person, I certainly can do so by proxy through the printed page.'

". . . . Jim, this is a pretty long letter. I write them once in awhile to my friends. They are known as 'Uncle Billy's love-letters.' I write them just as a word of cheer to the friend who has been laid aside for a little while. I am encouraged to write because no fellow who gets a Ridgway love-letter is under obligation to read it. If he throws it to one side, I will never know, and in the meantime, I have fulfilled part of my Boy Scout obligation in an attempt to do one of the two good turns which are my stunt every day!

"Trusting your sunset days will be the happiest of all your days, I remain as ever, with love,

"A friend of your youth,
"Bill"

The day before this letter was mailed, Mr. McConkey was taken with what seemed to be a heart attack. He

was unconscious through the day with apparently no
pain. At half-past four on Thursday morning, Sep-
tember 30, 1937, the spirit left its temporary dwelling-
place for the house not built with hands, for the City
which hath foundations! The transfer came so swiftly
that no loved one stood by at the passing, but while
there was no faithful Bedivere to clasp his hand at
the last, we know that the hand "clothed in white
samite, mystic, wonderful," or rather as he himself
would have said, "the blood-stained, nail-pierced
Hand," held his through the night watches, and then
as day began to dawn lifted him gently to the realm
where "there shall be no more death, neither sorrow,
nor crying, neither shall there be any more pain!"

For more than fifty years James McConkey struggled against physical limitations. He was spared after
all the other members of his family had passed on.
Not one of the sisters lived to such a ripe age as he.
While they all enjoyed better health than their brother,
they often prophesied that "Jim" would outlive all
of them because he guarded his health with such
scrupulous care. The prophecy proved to be correct.
We cannot believe, however, that length of days was
his portion solely because he took such excellent care
of his frail body. He was a chosen vessel, fit for the
Master's use. The Lord called him to do a great work,
and this piece of clay out of which the chosen
vessel was fashioned, was spared until the work was
accomplished.

No one knew how he suffered from the keen disappointment of baffled plans and the heartaches that
came when loved ones unspeakably precious to his soul
were torn from his presence. Nor would he speak of

temporal losses and broken fortunes that had stalked
into his life on account of the sin and wilfulness of
others. The long periods of separation from loved
ones and friends dearer to him than life, added to
his agony of soul and at times brought him to the
brink of broken faith. But in all these things he was
more than conqueror through Him who loves us. He
realized that nothing could separate him from the
love of God, and in this faith he trod the "highway
of victory." Through long years of chastening, he
learned what it meant to be yielded to the will of God.
He has told us in his own words: "It means more
than silver and gold; more than gratified desires and
ambition; more than all the sweet blandishments of
friendship; more than all the praises of men; more
than all the prizes of fame; yea, more than the attainment of all your highest earthly aims and strivings
is this richest and deepest of all blessings, to be hidden, sunken, swallowed up in the will of God for
all time and amid all circumstances." Truly, here
was a man who yielded his life to God with such com-
pleteness, such marvelous self-surrender that God gave
back to him his life wondrously enriched and glorified,
to be used as one of the most effective instruments of
this generation in carrying out the plan and purpose
of the Lord. So he went about doing good, redeeming
shattered lives, strengthening the weak, binding the
broken-hearted, speaking words of comfort and con-
solation to the bereaved, restoring the faith of count-
less multitudes, proclaiming the fathomless wealth of
the gospel of Christ, all because he knew that "he could
trust the Man who died for him."

The heart of his message, *The Threefold Secret*

of the Holy Spirit, might be given in these few
paragraphs quoted from the book in his opening chapter; after describing how water was supplied to a certain city from a reservoir and how a neighboring city
received its supply from a fountain of unlimited
abundance and marvelous beauty, he says:

"Even so it is with the life of the Holy Spirit in
God's children. Some have His indwelling life only
as a trickling stream with scarce enough to keep and
refresh them at times of test and stress, never knowing
what His fullness means. Others there are in whom the
words of Jesus are joyously fulfilled: 'I am come
that they might have life and that they might have it
more ABUNDANTLY' (more ABOUNDINGLY). Not only
are they filled with the Spirit in their own inner life
but they overflow in abundant, outgiving blessing to
the hungry and thirsty lives about that seek to know
the secret of their refreshing.

"There *is* a fullness of the Holy Ghost such as does
not come to most Christians at conversion, and there-
fore is, in point of time, usually a second experience.
But this is not the gift of the Holy Ghost, not the
receiving of the Holy Ghost, not the baptism of the
Holy Ghost as *God's Word* teaches. The Holy Ghost
is received once and forever at conversion. He is a
person. He comes in *then,* once and forever, and to *stay.*
We receive Him *then*—though we may not yield to
Him—for service, as well as for regeneration. At
Pentecost the Holy Ghost came down to form the
Church, the mystic body of Christ. On that great day
Christ baptized the church with the Holy Ghost.

"Let us therefore, when we have yielded our lives, be
grateful to God for such individual manifestation as

He may in His grace vouchsafe us. If He grants us wondrous visions, fills us with spiritual ecstasies, catches us up into the third heaven—it is well. But if He apportions to us a quieter experience; fills us with a peace as profound as other men's joy is rapturous; anoints us with power in prayer, instead of power in the pulpit:—this too is well. For He knows 'The Spirit divideth asunder severally as He will.'

" 'It is no longer I but *Christ that liveth in me,* and that life which I now live in the flesh, I live in faith.' Paul finds out that he is not only justified by faith but that the just must *live* by faith, not only that he has received the Spirit but that he must walk in the Spirit. He has reached the broadest conception of faith the believer can grasp—the faith of abiding. What then is this faith? It is that habitual attitude by which one who in himself is spiritually dead, is constantly looking to and daily and hourly drawing upon the life of another—the fullness of the life of Jesus Christ within him. This is the life of faith; this is the walk in the Spirit; this is abiding, on the Faith side of it.

"Beloved, do we realize that our *walk* in the Spirit is to be a constant, momentary *life* of faith as surely as our salvation was an act of faith? That we must not only be regenerated by faith, but live by faith? Do we believe that Christ meant exactly this when He said, 'Apart from me, ye can do *nothing*'? Dare we lead that meeting; write that paper or letter; make an address; hand out that tract; speak to that soul about Christ; make that decision; take that next step;—dare we do anything, without that swift uplift of faith to Him in whom alone dwelleth spiritual life? Have we

incarnated this fact of our own insufficiency into our
every-day Christian walk?

Faith is the gateway of communion with God;

Love, the gateway of ministry to men.

He who keeps them both constantly open has learned
to abide in Christ.

The believer is the temple of the Holy Ghost.

That temple is double-gated.

Faith is the gateway open God-ward.

Love is the gateway open man-ward.

Through Faith, the Divine life, so to speak, flows
into us;

Through Love, it flows out to others.

Faith is the channel of communion with God;

Love, the channel of ministry to men.

God desires not only to pour His life *into* us through
Faith;

But through us to others through Love."

XV

AFTERWARDS

WHILE the dust was returning to dust in the family plot of Fairview Cemetery, in Wrightsville, tributes about the way this man of God had been used in their lives were being received from men and women far and near. We shall quote from a few of these:

"I received untold blessing from his writings, especially *The Threefold Secret of the Holy Spirit*." —CHAS. G. TRUMBULL, Editor, Sunday School Times

"My thought of him centers around his marvelous love and loyalty to Christ, a love that has stood tests most demanding in his latter years. I also think of Him as a man of unique ability as an author. His writings have gone to the ends of the earth and never have they failed to be a transforming blessing. It would not be possible to estimate in this world what has been accomplished by *The Threefold Secret of the Holy Spirit* or by his book on prayer. All of this wonderful setting forth of truth is made doubly effective by Mr. McConkey's pure and fragrant life. Probably but few are now living who knew him in his earlier years when his physical strength supported his rare spirit and devotion to Christ. He is ever to be known as a great Christian."—LEWIS SPERRY CHAFER, President, Dallas Theological Seminary

"As I contemplate my uncle's life, I instinctively think of the unremitting pressure of pain and suffering that weighed upon him with such painful intensity during most of the years of his earthly pilgrimage. A man of lesser faith and without the spiritual reserves that he possessed would have been utterly crushed and embittered. I am convinced that it was primarily by this thorn in the flesh that the Lord revealed to James McConkey the riches of His grace and enabled him to be a great overcomer. His prayer life opened heaven's windows. Through them he saw so clearly the open secret of God's will that nothing could turn him aside from a complete surrender of his life to the Lord.

"The outward man has perished but the spirit lives on and with him will live his testimony to the love and power of Jesus Christ, whose he was and whom he served. . . . It may be difficult to give a comprehensive definition of spirituality, but whoever enjoyed the privilege of intimate friendship with James McConkey was conscious of a presence that completely lifted him above mundane things. I know of no man who ever made spirituality so real to me as my uncle."

—W. McCONKEY KERR, York, Pa.

"First of all, he had a heart for God, redeemed, renewed, sanctified; then, a heart for his fellow-men that they too might know his Savior."—O. R. PALMER, Pastor Berachah Church, Philadelphia

"My first contact with James McConkey was during my student days. I attended a district conference which was held at Franklin and Marshall College, Lancaster, Pennsylvania, where he was the guest speaker. He impressed me during those days with his humility, his intelligence and his consecration. I felt that here was a man who 'walked with God,' and a man to whom the Spirit had revealed the deep things of God. His messages to us on *The Surrendered Life* led me to a life of deeper fellowship with our Lord. Later I had the privilege of hearing him again at the Y.M.C.A. conference at Eaglesmere, Pennsylvania. God used his messages on the Holy Spirit to lead us into the life more abundant where Christ is Master and Lord.

"When I went to Africa as a missionary, I had with me his book, *Prayer*. Next to the Word itself, this has been to me the most helpful in the development of my prayer life. At one of our field conferences, I used it as the basis of our morning devotions to the profit of all.

"On one of my later furloughs it was again my privilege to sit at his feet and listen to his heart-searching, soul-stirring, Christ-exalting messages. His was a Spirit-filled life of joy, power, and fruitfulness. To him I owe a great debt of gratitude for no other person has so deeply influenced my life as James McConkey."—C. W. GUINTER, Pastor Grace Evangelical Church, Wrightsville, Pa.

"One of God's noblemen!"—JOHN B. GORDON, Pastor, Presbyterian Church, Timmonsville, Pa.

"I love 'Brother Jim' and delight to see his memory honored. The earliest recollection I have of him was back in the early nineties when he was engaged in teaching a circuit of Bible classes among railroad men. Hundreds of them were led to Christ and into fruitful Christian service through his ministry.

"Once in Florida, I learned that he was at Jackson-ville teaching in a church there. I routed my return northward to spend Wednesday night in the city, hoping I might see him, that being prayer meeting night. When I reached the church, it was a full half-hour before meeting time and I found him there all alone. I had not seen him or heard from him for fourteen years but when, in the dimly lighted room, I grasped his hand, he said, 'Brother William, I have been praying for you all day! Less than an hour ago I was on my knees praying for you.' You may imagine how his words warmed my heart.

"He was a truly great man—a rich gift to the Church of God in a day when such men are sorely needed. We thank our God upon every remembrance of him." —WILLIAM L. PETTINGILL.

At Bethany House, in Pittsburgh, the comfortable mansion now used as a Bible teaching center and as a home for missionaries on furlough, a memorial service was held on October 1, the day after his death. This was fitting for although Mr. McConkey had never crossed the threshold of Bethany, the whole place bears testimony to God's use of his messages in the lives of all those connected with the House. Photographs of him are in evidence everywhere, supplies of his books and tracts are kept in the library and the room later designated as "the prophet's chamber" was then called "Mr. McConkey's room." He had never been able to enjoy this spacious first-floor room because the house had not been occupied until after his illness, but daily, individual prayer and weekly, united prayer that he might be enabled to spend his last years under this roof went up from all the friends there, who felt that his mere presence would be a benediction to the place.

At this simple memorial service were gathered many of those who had felt the power of God go out from this man's life, who had been constrained by the working of the Spirit through him to yield their lives also. Miss Edith Nelson said afterwards that one of her family urged her to stay in that night on account of a cold but she replied, "Not go to the memorial service of Brother James—the best friend I ever had!"

After prayer and praise, that evening, some informal testimonies were given about the way in which he had been used in the lives of those present. Mr. Clark M. Kefover, Mr. Frank S. Gardner, Mr. A. N. Fraser, Dr. Thomas Miller, Mr. W. G. A. Millar, Mr. C. H. Lehman, who have proven the power of Christ in business circles of Pittsburgh, told of how they had learned the secret from James H. McConkey and how they had seen all his teaching exemplified in his own life.

Within a few days following this meeting, suggestions came from three different friends widely separated, that Bethany House, in Pittsburgh, be made a memorial to Mr. McConkey. Letters from other friends followed and after much prayer and waiting on God, the editors of *Christ Life* magazine (now published by Bethany House) announced that it had been decided to do this.

Wherever the news of his death had been received, expressions rose from those who had known and loved him. A business man in Richmond who had seen him in the daily round but had not had opportunity to hear much of his teaching said, "If there's a Better Place for mortals to go, then I know Mr. McConkey

is there; and if he is not there, there's no use for the
rest of us to try to go!"

Through all the tributes received, whether from those
of low or high degree, ran one golden thread—the
thread of love. Theologians recognized and appreciated his keen, spiritual discernment and powerful
logic, but they, as well as untaught Christians, realized
the fact that, after all, the most powerful, pungent
factor in all his testimony was love—love for God and
love for man. Without this, his sound teaching clothed
in literary excellence would have had no power to draw
the hearts of men. It was this loving-ness that drew
them to him and it was his all-absorbing love for his
Lord which made them feel as he spoke that he was
right, that it *was* worth while to surrender everything
to Him.

Doubtless every Christian covets a wealth of human
love such as was lavished upon James McConkey but
few realize what it costs. For years, he had shunned
even an unloving thought as some would shun only a
criminal one. He had seized every opportunity to
enter into the personal interests of men, to encourage
them and to pray through their problems with them.
He had not spared his time and strength for what
might have seemed inconsequential contacts. He had
let his own affairs sink into obscurity while all his
attention was riveted on the affairs of those he was
trying to win. He had lost himself and thereby saved
for himself undying friendship in the hearts of all
whom he knew intimately. One is reminded of the
story he used to tell about the godly engineer, Jim,
who had faithfully given his testimony to the president of his railroad and was on his deathbed when his

chief said to him, "Jim, I would give all I have if I could say as you do, 'I know that my Redeemer lives,' " and Jim replied, "Mr. President, that's just what it cost me!"

Once, when he had mentioned something about giving a message in his old home-church, he remarked, "I don't know that I am a prophet honored in my own country, but the people of Wrightsville have certainly shown kindness to me." Now that he has gone, the townspeople may not fully realize the greatness of the man who went from their midst but they know the genuineness of his Christian character. One of his old acquaintances in Wrightsville remarked to Mr. Charles Kerr on the day before the funeral, "There's no use in having his funeral preached. Everybody around here knew what he was. His life was his funeral sermon!"

Yes, and his books are his monument. Those who have felt the touch of the gentle hand and have seen the light of love in the gray-blue eyes can never read them without connecting the man with the message, but those who never knew the man and later generations which will never have a chance to know him in the flesh, still can feel something of the wealth of love which went from his heart into the very printed page, rise to meet their own.

He was only a piece of clay that the Lord used, only a voice in the wilderness proclaiming the loveliness of his Lord and gently but firmly pressing on men His claim upon their lives. The response they gave to the message caused his soul the deepest satisfaction it ever knew, and as we feebly try to envision him in the glory-world, our minds can think of nothing, aside from the consciousness of the personal presence of his Savior, that would add more to his joys already infinite than to watch the movement of the messages he has left behind.

I feel quite confident that he never spent any anxious hours in the fear that men would look at him and not at his Lord. That thought never seemed to occur to him—it would have been too absurd. He knew the message was clear and that was all that counted— to make it so clear that men would accept it. His only thought for the messenger was that he might have their brotherly love, that was all; but those who knew his heart realized how bitterly disappointed he would have been if they *had* looked upon him as anything except a fellow-Christian and since his going, when little groups of friends meet and talk about him, it is noticeable how they shun anything that savors of the glorification of the man. One of them, a man who has perhaps a wider acquaintance with the highest type of Christian leaders than any other man in Richmond, remarked just after his death, "I know a great many Bible teachers and Christian leaders, but I have never known one that lived any closer—nor as close—to the Lord as Brother James did." And everyone who heard him say it knew that there was no glorification-of-the-flesh here, that what this man had done, any other Christian could do, provided the life were yielded!

If, by any stretch of the imagination, one could envision him as writing an autobiography, we would feel quite sure about the facts he would emphasize. When enthusiastic readers of his books clamored for information about the author, he submitted to the publishing of *A Word About the Author*, a one-page leaflet sent out by the Silver Publishing Society. On this were mentioned the factors which he considered most important in the making of his life — his mother, Princeton, broken health and baffled plans, opportunities afforded by Y.M.C.A.'s for teaching, Mr. Kelker, itinerant Bible teaching, the Silver Publishing Society, and the Braille Circulating Library. He could have written the story of his life on a dozen pages and would have thought it entirely adequate for, in his opinion, there was only one important act in his life— one upon which everything else hinged—and that was the acceptance of Jesus Christ as his Savior and the presenting of his body a living sacrifice, holy, acceptable unto God—his reasonable service!

Printed in United States of America